19.50

GEORGE MEREDITH

GEORGE MEREDITH

A Reappraisal of the Novels

Mohammad Shaheen

Barnes & Noble Books
Totowa, New Jersey

First published 1981 by
THE MACMILLAN PRESS LTD
London and Basingstoke
Companies and representatives
throughout the world

First published in the USA 1981 by
BARNES & NOBLE BOOKS
81, Adams Drive
Totowa, New Jersey

Printed in Hong Kong

British Library Cataloguing in Publication Data

Shaheen, Mohammad
  George Meredith
  1. Meredith, George, b.1828 – Criticism and
  interpretation
  823'.8   PR5014

MACMILLAN ISBN 0–333–24007–3

BARNES & NOBLE ISBN 0–389–20022–0

TO

S.J.C.

'Were I a dashing writer of railway prose or even a composer of practical flimsy, this would not matter; but I write studying . . .'

The Letters of George Meredith (I, 505)

Contents

Preface

This book consists of an introduction and six chapters. The introduction gives an account of the thematic and technical issues which are explored in the body of the book. The six chapters have as their unifying theme Meredith's effort to exploit the art of the novel as a flexible instrument for recording personal and social experience.

References to *The Ordeal of Richard Feverel* are to the Riverside Edition, edited by C. L. Cline (New York: 1971). References to other works of Meredith, not otherwise specified, are to the Memorial Edition, 27 vols (London: 1909–11). Chapter and page number are used for the text referred to or quoted.

The main source of the unpublished material used in this book is the *Altschul Collection*, Beinecke Rare Book and Manuscript Library, Yale University Library.

The place of publication in all references not otherwise specified is London.

To Mrs Gillian Beer I am indebted not only for her friendship and writings over many years but also for her help, advice and criticism during the time which was spent in the preparation of this book. I am also grateful to Dr Patrick Parrinder, whose criticism of my work was invaluable. Mr A. R. Milburn and Mr Wilfrid Lockwood kindly read through the text. I am especially grateful to Professor Ian Fletcher whose criticism of the chapter on *Harry Richmond* was constructive and invaluable.

I owe a particular debt to the Curators of Yale University Library, the Pierpont Morgan Library and to King's College Library, Cambridge, for allowing me to use and occasionally quote from the unpublished material in their care.

A special debt of gratitude is to Mr and Mrs Derek O. New for their unfailing encouragement during my stay in Cambridge.

In conclusion I would like to thank the University of Jordan for making available research funds.

M.S.

Acknowledgements

The author and publishers wish to thank the following who have kindly given permission for the use of copyright material: Houghton Mifflin Company, for the extracts from *George Meredith: The Ordeal of Richard Feverel*, edited by and with introduction and notes by C. L. Cline. Riverside Editions. Copyright © 1971 by C. L. Cline; Oxford University Press, for the extracts from *Letters of George Meredith*, edited by C. L. Cline (1970); Murray Pollinger, on behalf of Jack Lindsay, for the extracts from *George Meredith: His Life and Work*, reprinted by Kraus-Thomson Organization Ltd; the University of Nebraska-Lincoln, for the extracts from *Art and Substance in George Meredith* by Walter Wright. Copyright © 1953 by the University of Nebraska Press; and A. P. Watt Ltd, on behalf of the Estate of H. G. Wells, for the extracts from *The Story of a Great Schoolmaster*.

1 Introduction

In a controversy over whether to admit Meredith to the Cambridge English syllabus, two fundamental questions were raised in the pages of the *Times Literary Supplement* in 1960.[1] The first question was the extent to which Meredith's novels are Victorian. André Gomme placed him among 'the more Victorian Victorians', and consequently suggested that one of his novels would be just enough for undergraduates 'to find out for themselves why they cannot afford the time for more'. The second question was raised by W. J. Lucas, who, in response to this antipathy, asked Gomme which novel he would have them read pointing out that Meredith's fiction varies from one novel to another. He concludes: 'It could as well be argued that one has only to read "The Lake Isle of Innisfree" to see that Yeats is a minor poet of a singularly unrewarding kind.'

After the appearance of his first novel, *The Ordeal of Richard Feverel*, Meredith confronted a hostile reaction from the public because of the alleged immorality of the novel. He was distressed that Mudie, after ordering five hundred copies for his circulating library, suppressed the book from his reading list. Meredith wrote to Samuel Lucas: 'O canting Age! I predict a Deluge. Mudie is Metternich: and after him—. Meantime I am tabooed from all decent drawing-room tables.' (I, 39) He told Samuel Lucas that the book would not attract a second reading: 'At least not among newspaper critics— to whom all honour and glory.'

After this setback, Meredith, driven by financial necessity, embarked in the 1860s on an attempt to reconcile his artistic bent to the taste of the reading public. His first book in this period was *Evan Harrington*. This was serialised in *Once a Week*, of which Lucas was editor. Meredith's anxiety over the reception of the novel is seen in his correspondence with Lucas. While working on the book he wrote: 'But Oh! Heaven! Why have you advertised me as a "popular author"? Isn't it almost a fraud on the public? Won't they stare when they behold this notorious child they are quite

---

Unless otherwise stated, all references to the letters are to C. L. Cline's edition (Oxford, 1970).

unacquainted with?' (I, 48) In another letter written while the book
was running in serial, Meredith wrote: 'Read and let me have your
opinion. It develops the character of the hero partly: the incidents
subsequently affect him. But I wish to know how you take it. It does
not much move the tale. But do not insist on that entirely, at
present.' (I, 49)

  Evan Harrington was designed to combine the popular themes of
snobbery and romantic comedy. The picture of the Countess de
Saldar is reminiscent of Becky Sharp of *Vanity Fair*, and the
portrayal of the Cogglesby brothers and Mr John Raikes come close
to Dickens's comic figures. The result is low comedy.

  The second novel of this experimental period was *Emilia in
England*, in which Meredith turned to a wider range of theme and
character in his attempt to win popularity. The novel offers that
ever-popular form of fiction, historical narrative while at the same
time it tries to avoid what the public had found unacceptable in
Evan Harrington and immoral in *The Ordeal*. Meredith wrote to the
American publisher Harper: 'The present volume is of a different
texture, [from *Evan Harrington*] and will not offend as *The Ordeal of
Richard Feverel* is said to have done.' (I, 234) *Emilia*, however, neither
satisfied its author nor won popularity for him. To Dr Jessop he wrote
(May 1864) that he was 'unpleasant in review style' and that he 'gets
slaps from the reviewers' for having written *Emilia*. (I, 255)

  In his next work, *Rhoda Fleming*, Meredith tried to find a balance
between theme and character by introducing many incidents of an
improbable nature such as to allow scope for the delineation of
character. The result, however, was a melodrama which was even
less well-received by the reviewers than *Emilia* had been.

  Meredith then returned to *Vittoria*, a sequel to *Emilia* which he
had started earlier but put aside in order to write *Rhoda Fleming*, a
work 'of the real story-telling order'. (I, 250) In *Vittoria* (or *Emilia in
Italy*), Meredith exploits his knowledge of Italy, and on one
occasion asked his friend, Wyse, to stay with him in order to help
with some Italian 'local colourism'. (I, 276–7) But local colour did
not please the reviewers as Meredith had hoped. One review, for
example, commented: '*Vittoria* is a tale of the manqué Italian
Revolution of 1849, by Mr George Meredith, an author hitherto
known as a novelist of some ability and a rather low ethical tone.'[2]
Though, like *Emilia*, *Vittoria* was a sensationalised presentation of
history, it did achieve wider circulation and a better sale than its
predecessors.

The foregoing brief account of Meredith's fiction in the sixties is intended not to disparage these novels, which do provide special interest for particular researchers, but rather to indicate that it was not within Meredith's capacity to become 'Victorian' even when he attempted to conform to public taste. His novels of the sixties were destined not to win popularity, though as experiments they contributed towards the further development of his fiction.

In the 1870s Meredith gave rein to his artistic bent and, consequently, remained unpopular with the reading public. In the eighties, he again courted public taste, though now with more confidence in his art, and reached the peak of his popularity with *Diana of the Crossways*, a novel cast in the biographical form which was currently popular. The achievement of popularity did not, however, lead Meredith to continue writing in the same vein. *One of Our Conquerors*, his next novel, made no concessions to public taste, and it is Meredith's most difficult as well as most typical work. Its condemnation by reviewers led him to write *Lord Ormont and his Aminta*, which has a thematic pattern similar to the preceding and following works, but a much simpler presentation of character. The result was a story of more popular appeal but which gave less satisfaction to its author. *The Amazing Marriage*, Meredith's last complete novel, reconciled what pleased the public with the author's own purpose through the two-fold function of romance in the novel, but it did not win Meredith any considerable popularity; and his audience remained limited until the end of his literary career.

The development of Meredith's fiction which extended over the last three decades of the century, and the wide range of purpose explored in the novels, caused W. J. Lucas to ask which one novel epitomised Meredith's art. Gomme, in reply to Lucas, chose either *The Egoist*, which he thought 'represents Meredith at his best', or *Beauchamp's Career*, which he believed 'would do equally well'. Such an argument overlooks the fact that, although both novels were written during the same period, each introduces us to a different Meredith.

Gomme's choice, however, is not unusual in modern criticism. E. M. Forster, by whom Gomme is clearly influenced, illustrated his criticism of Meredith in *Aspects of the Novel* mainly from *The Egoist* and partly from *Beauchamp's Career*. In an unpublished lecture, Forster chose *The Egoist*: on this occasion to illustrate the civilisation of the pre-war period, since he takes Meredith to be representative of that era, in contrast to Proust and Auden who are taken as representative of the twenties and thirties respectively.[3]

It has been common practice in modern criticism to approach Meredith mainly through *The Egoist* and to consider him a writer of comedy and anatomist of egoism. Christopher Caudwell, for example, writes that 'not only *The Egoist*, but all Meredith's books are about egoists and careerists. . .'.[4] The main reason for this judgement comes from the direct relevance of the novel to the only critical document that Meredith produced: *An Essay on Comedy and the Comic Spirit*. The essay, too, bears similar relevance to Meredith's short fiction.

These works of the late seventies are presumably the only body of Meredith's writings where the critic can apply theory to practice. This perhaps explains why *The Egoist* has received more critical discussion than any other of Meredith's novels, and why critics have been tempted to extend the comic interpretation backward to *The Ordeal* and forward to *The Amazing Marriage*. An example is Joseph Warren Beach's study: *The Comic Spirit in George Meredith*. Such criticism forces on Meredith's work an interpretation which applies only to one stage of his development. It ignores the fact that Meredith himself realised the limitation of comedy when he wrote to R. L. Stevenson that he yearned to have finished *The Egoist* because 'it came mainly from the head and had nothing to kindle imagination'. (II, 573) Meredith 'thirsted to be rid of it soon after conception', when he realised that the idea of comedy epitomised the spirit of the time.

Comedy is the only aspect of Meredith that can be described as Victorian, in that the comic spirit is basically a moral power and comedy deals with deviations from the norm of society. However, neither the popularity of *The Egoist* nor its success in catching the tone of society satisfied Meredith, and as soon as he had finished it he began *The Amazing Marriage* as a recast of *The Egoist*.

The Egoist then is typical of Meredith only in a limited sense. What is especially typical of him is the continual development of his fiction. Unlike many of his fellow Victorian novelists, Meredith was not concerned to justify himself to reviewers and readers through critical introductions or prefaces. His criticism as it exists consists of scattered remarks, of which most are interpolated in the novels themselves, the rest in his letters and reports to Chapman and Hall as a publisher's reader. But these remarks form no coherent critical theory and at the same time they lack the technicality of criticism.

David Daiches once said that 'Meredith is the most difficult Victorian writer to come to critical terms with.'[5] This comment raises the most crucial problem of how to approach Meredith critically, and acknowledges Meredith to be deserving of more serious study than would be granted by those who dismissed him from the 'great tradition' and were reluctant to admit him to the curriculum of the Cambridge English school.

The present study is an attempt to provide a critical assessment of Meredith's fiction and hopes to bring readers and critics to closer terms with the author and his world of fiction. Five novels are chosen for this purpose: *The Ordeal of Richard Feverel*, *The Adventures of Harry Richmond*, *Beauchamp's Career*, *One of Our Conquerors*, and *The Amazing Marriage*. They are selected as being more representative than other novels of Meredith's independent mind, in that they were written with less concern for popularity. Although each novel is examined as a study in itself, similar patterns of theme and character are explored to show how Meredith combined the diverse elements of his fiction.

In describing the thematic and technical issues explored in the study I am aware that some simplification is involved, and would like to remind the reader of not attributing to such terms as are used any clear definitive capacity. Theme, for example, may be used to indicate the author's implied norm, or may simply mean the objective of the book, otherwise referred to as the author's purpose.

The question explored in this study is not the identification of theme but rather how the theme is presented in character. The study holds that theme and character are inextricably mingled and the theme acquires specificity only through character. A common practice which this study hopes to counter is the tendency to abstract a theme, or certain themes, for the evaluation of Meredith's work. Meredith's reputation has suffered from the tendency of contemporary reviewers and critics arbitrarily to select a theme which fits their own critical view. It is regrettable that this practice should continue in modern criticism. Donald Fanger, for example, sorts out themes in which, he claims, Meredith found an expression of his view of life in general and a reflection of his personal life. Fanger parallels the father–son relationship with Arthur's upbringing, the unhappy marriage with Meredith's first marriage, the constricting role of social convention with the shame of his origin, money as a social lever with his grave need of money, and egoism and sentimentality in the novels with Meredith's own. Fanger concludes that 'Meredith's chief compulsion was what he would have called "loquency": he could not stop talking in company or in his books . . . even long enough to hear himself.'[6]

Concentration on theme has often led to the conclusion that Meredith's works are repetitive. Typical of this trend is V. S. Pritchett's criticism. It is true, as Pritchett says, that Meredith's novels are essentially stories of an education, and that in *Richard Feverel*, in *Evan Harrington*, in *Harry Richmond*, in *Beauchamp's Career* and in *The Egoist*, 'the hero has to unlearn by passing through an ordeal and, when he is stripped naked, has painfully to build upon his new, strange self-knowledge'.[7] Such a thematic account lacks that perceptive reading of character which would lead to the realisation that education in the books mentioned is a façade. Being itself repetitive, Pritchett's criticism of Meredith over the last two decades has not penetrated behind this façade.

A similar practice is that of grouping together characters from various novels as types on the basis of similar traits that can be traced in them. In the course of her study Gwendolyn O. Stewart remarks that:

> Princess Ottilia, Harry's first love, provides an example of an immature, romantic girl, while Janet Ilchester, whom Harry finally marries, belongs to the Rose Jocelyn category. In *Beauchamp's Career* Cecilia Halkett is similar to Ottilia and Jenny Denham resembles Janet. As would be expected, both Ottilia and Cecilia lack guidance, their immaturities parallel those of Harry and Beauchamp, whose growth is remarked by Janet and Jenny.[8]

It is the main concern of this study to demonstrate that the purpose of each novel selected lies in its exploring the individuality of character and not in its presentation of topicality of theme or typicality of character. To provide a comprehensive picture of the way character is individualised a detailed character analysis of each novel is given. It is hoped to establish that development in Meredith's fiction can be traced in the individuality revealed by each character and not in a thematic unity arbitrarily imposed on Meredith's fiction. Before I proceed to the scrutiny of the novels themselves I propose to give a brief account of the various aspects of characterisation explored later in the body of this study.

In his letter to Bainton (September 1887) Meredith wrote: 'I do not make a plot. If my characters as I have them at heart before I begin on them, were boxed into a plot, they would soon lose the lines of their features.' (II, 888) Meredith's disregard of plot as a sequence of incidents arranged in time appears in various forms throughout his writings. The external unity of the narrative is kept at a minimum in the novels. In the first revision of *The Ordeal* (1878) Meredith compressed the first four chapters of the book into one, eliminating much of the introductory history of Sir Austin's system. Beauchamp's past career occupies one chapter (IV). *One of Our Conquerors* begins with internal action, and incidents come to us refracted through the consciousness of character right from the opening sentence. The history of Carinthia and her brother is given in the first four chapters of *The Amazing Marriage*.

Meredith deliberately avoided the popular straightforward exposition of narrative. His contemporary readers found it difficult to follow the crippled story whose events occur in fragments and whose incidents are presented as allusions. However, plot in Meredith's fiction remains loose only in the sense of falling short of providing a flowing narrative. It has its own unity which springs from character. Forster credited Meredith with what his contemporaries failed to recognise, and his description of plot in Meredith is, I think, most ingenious when he says that. 'A Meredithian plot . . . resembles a series of kiosks most artfully placed among wooded slopes, which his people reach by their own impetus, and from which they emerge with altered aspect. Incident springs out of character, and having occurred it alters that character. People and events are closely connected, and he does it by means of these contrivances.'[9]

Action in Meredith's fiction is what he describes in connection with *Harry Richmond* as 'actions of the mind'. In one of his letters he refers to it as 'the natural history of the soul'. (II, 876) Words are deeds. Characters are revealed to us by what they say rather than by what they do. We know them through their comtemplative selves. Meredith's heroes are all brought back from the battlefield to embark on a new heroism—the heroism of the mind. In *The Ordeal* he alludes mockingly to an audience impatient for blood and glory in fiction; in *Beauchamp's Career* he warns the reader that his characters 'conquer nothing, win none' (XLVIII, 553); and Victor of *One of Our Conquerors* achieves no victory.

Character and action can be identified as motive and deed, or what Meredith describes in *Diana of the Crossways* as man's rationalised image of himself and his self in action. (I, 19) In *Beauchamp's Career* Meredith says that ideas are actually the motives of men. (I, 7) Motive then can be described as the impulse which drives the individual to test the existence (or the validity) of his idea. The two prevailing ideas in Meredith's fiction are nature and egoism in proportions which vary from one character and occasion to another. For this reason I propose to leave them without definitive description here.

Character and action on the one hand correlate with the ideal and the actual on the other. The friction between them is the most characteristic feature in the development of character in Meredith's fiction, and this study shows how variable in structure and intensity the conflict is. In *The Ordeal* there are two different motives in Sir Austin: one is his love for his son, another is the egoism originating from his anger with his wife. The action is supposedly carried out through the system of education adopted by Sir Austin for his son's upbringing. Meredith's design for the purpose of the book as revealed in his letter to Lucas (I, 40) is that the System fails and the tragedy happens because of the discrepancy between the two motives. The study of *The Ordeal* shows that the main flaw in its design comes out of Meredith's confusion over the total correspondence between motive and action, and a close examination of the book will show that the father's egoism is never actually tested to the conclusion that love is overcome by egoism. Meredith's theory of the design remains itself untested.

A serious preoccupation for Meredith in his early writings was to relate character to action and to explain one in terms of another. While his second novel *Evan Harrington* was appearing as a serial he wrote to Lucas: 'This cursed desire I have haunting me to show the reasons for things is a perpetual obstruction to movement.' (I, 57) In the 1860s he continued to be haunted by this desire which reached its limit in *Rhoda Fleming*.

With *Harry Richmond* the problem of internal consistency between character and action is solved through the evolving nature of their design. The driving force in Harry to explore his relationship with the world at large (not with society) is tested against time and experience. Conflict in the book emerges with the evolution of Harry's mind. However, conflict in *Harry Richmond* remains limited because the division in Harry is between his individual desires, or, to use a stock term used for the criticism of the nineteenth century intellectual background, between will and necessity. The conflict is resolved by the reconciliation of one desire to another, and it is the only one of Meredith's novels where the conflict is happily resolved.

The last three novels show how conflict becomes more complex as the individual self acquires social and political drives. In *Beauchamp's Career* the conflict is between the ideal of the individual and the actuality of society. Here the ideal in Beauchamp (whether related to his own affairs or to public life) conflicts with the actual outside. The conflict grows more complex in *One of Our Conquerors* because both sides are internal. In *The Amazing Marriage* conflict grows even more complex as the distance between the ideal and actual becomes less, for Fleetwood is capable of putting the ideal into practice briefly, but remains in conflict because he is incapable of sustaining this state of affairs. Fleetwood lives with both nature and egoism in him as contraries.

The degree of complexity may be viewed in the light of the perspective envisaged in each novel. In *Beauchamp's Career* reconciliation would have been possible had society been responsive; in *One of Our Conquerors* resolution of conflict appears to be less possible because the ideal is counteracted both by the actual in Victor and the same 'actual' in society; and in *The Amazing Marriage* the possibility of reconciliation becomes elusive.

Though Meredith was writing outside the field of popular fiction (at least in the five novels selected) he was not unaware of current critical issues related to narration; but as usual he expressed his concern for them in his own way. In an early review he wrote: 'After a satisfactory construction of plot, when to dramatise and when to narrate is the novelist's question.'[10] In his unpublished *Notebook* he wrote: 'The first point in studying others is to be disengaged from ourselves.'[11]

On various other occasions Meredith expressed his awareness of what is generally known as the point of view or the aesthetic distance. It is what W. J. Harvey describes as the sense of implied reality which centres around a certain axis in the novel, and the second is simply the mode of narration.[12] The interpretation of Meredith's writings has often suffered from the arbitrary emphasis which results from the adoption of a particular point of view.

Meredith confronts the question of aesthetic distance right from the beginning, and the discussion of *The Ordeal* points to the inadequate control over sympathy with and detachment from character as he compounds tragedy with comedy. The discussion examines the interaction of two norms. The thematic norm of the novel is the recounting of the ordeal of father and son which is in origin autobiographical. Comedy, which provides a technical norm, is designed to rationalise the situation by controlling the excessive emotionality of the ordeal. But the ordeal grows in intensity, and laughter at father and son becomes ill-placed. The discussion shows that Meredith embarked on a bifurcating course in intensifying the ordeal while at the same time rationalising it. The resulting disruption of norm is accompanied by diversity in the narrative.

Harry Richmond shows how Meredith exploits the *Bildungsroman* so as to gain control over aesthetic distance. It points to Meredith's success in defining the relationship between reader and narrator (who is the character) as well as among characters themselves. Rationalisation, another point emphasised in the discussion, is handed over to character (Harry and Ottilia).

In *Beauchamp's Career* emphasis is placed on the way Meredith fulfills the promise presented in the two interpolated critical passages. It demonstrates Meredith's concern for the sense of illusion as implied in the detachment of narrator from character. The interpolations ask the reader to acknowledge in advance the wilful individuality of Beauchamp in controlling the narrative from beginning to end. The discussion of the novel points to Meredith's aim of orienting the reader to accept Beauchamp in his suffering without at the same time contriving a character who attracts sympathy.

In *One of Our Conquerors* Meredith makes no apology for the proximity of narrator and character, and on several points in the narrative an approximate parallel can be established to the stream of consciousness. Instead of the detachment between character and narrator as in the previous novel, the discussion of this novel explores the individual character's attempt to detach himself from his own suffering by exploiting language and music.

Narration in *The Amazing Marriage* is carried out through an elaborate device which solves the question of when to narrate and when to dramatise. Dame Gossip is trusted with the first side while the narrator takes the other. The critical analysis of the design explains the necessity of the rivalry between the two in preventing the domination of the whole narrative by either. The aesthetic distance extends over the joint effort of narration.

The question of where the sense of reality lies is thus shown to be misleading. In each novel there is traced and scrutinised a revelatory situation, a passage or an allusion which usually occurs towards the end. In *The Ordeal* it is the letter of Lady Blandish, but as Lady Blandish is referred to earlier as sentimental her condemnation of Sir Austin cannot be accepted as the focal point of view, and in Wayne Booth's description she would be an unreliable commentator. The reader is left in uncertainty. In *Harry Richmond* the point of view comes in a form of retrospective recognition when Ottilia, who is a reliable commentator, expresses her distrust of the validity of the rational mind to Harry. In *Beauchamp's Career* Dr Shrapnel and Lord Romfrey, the two extreme characters of the novel, join together in retrospective recognition as they regret the loss of Beauchamp to England. It is not until this revelation that we know that the narrator's sympathy lies with the ideal which Beauchamp lived with and for. In *One of our Conquerors* the last sentence tells us that egoism in Victor should receive no condemnation by the narrator because he and Nataly together kept faith with nature. In *The Amazing Marriage* we know in retrospect that Fleetwood was genuinely and seriously attracted by Carinthia when he proposed to her, and the narrator's sympathy with character is similarly suggested by the abstinence from condemning Fleetwood's egoism.

The study argues particularly against the kind of criticism which overlooks the revelatory occasions in the novels and consequently misrepresents their purpose. Moreover, it traces the common source for the misrepresentation of purpose which tends to take the ending of the novel in the light of an established norm of society. In this case the result is moral generalisation of theme and a failure to see the theme in its proper perspective.

Walter Wright, for example, categorises Meredith's writings in accordance with their endings into romance, comedy, tragicomedy, and tragedy. As he approaches *The Ordeal* he comments: 'From the vantage point of the tragic ending we judge both the framework of the novel and the qualities which make the story significant.'[13] Another example which, because of its typicality, receives detailed discussion here, is Norman Kelvin's criticism of Meredith. Kelvin reduces Meredith's writings to a conflict of the rational and the irrational in society and individual. He views the life of the individual character as a quest for the reconciliation with the rational. In *Harry Richmond* I argue against Kelvin's claim that the reconciliation between Harry and Janet suggests the triumph of rational mind which they acquire through their contact with Ottilia. The study continues to argue against similar claims applied to other novels.

Parallel to Kelvin's critical outlook is a recent study by Donald Stone. He takes Meredith to be mainly concerned with the demonstration of the Victorian ideal of responsibility and altruistic individualism. The conflict, he observes, is designed to lead the individual to find a way of accommodating his altruism in society. He claims that Meredith fails after *The Egoist*, as the focus on this ideal is lost and his style becomes difficult. Typical of his confusion over theme and character is the following comment: 'The most memorable of Meredith's creations are his irrationals, hopelessly unteachable—the Countess de Saldar, Sir Willoughby Pattern, and Richmond Roy. And it is the depiction of an irrational society, as in *Beauchamp's Career* or *One of Our Conquerors*, which is still accessible to generations that have long ago stopped believing in intellectual progress.'[14]

Another critical performance which exemplifies the misreading of Meredith's purpose is that of Jack Lindsay's, who claims that Meredith's fiction is mainly concerned with exposing a cash-nexus society and its destructive power. Despite his dogmatic approach to the novels, Lindsay's study of the background of the novels remains the most perceptive of its kind. Lindsay's analysis of *Beauchamp's Career* and *One of Our Conquerors* shows, I think, that Lindsay's approach, like that of other critics mentioned above, has the limitation of overlooking the dynamic force of character.

I have attempted to demonstrate that Meredith is not concerned with dignifying the ego or demolishing necessity, but rather with presenting the interlocking forces of the two in action.

From among Meredith's scattered critical comments two general remarks can be extracted: one is Meredith's belief in a synthesis between idealism and realism, another, which is not separable from the first, lies in his conception of realism as a state of mind (usually one of disillusionment) rather than a technique of objective presentation. This attitude is close to Ford's 'certain tang of disillusionment as to the motives of mankind'.

Interaction between romance and realism represented for Meredith an alternation of two states of mind: one is general, the other is specific. This situation is demonstrated in *Harry Richmond*.

In his later novels, as individual characters become socially involved, the identification moves from simple to complex states of consciousness. Here realism, as Gillian Beer describes it, 'will show the continuity between man in society and man in the depths below consciousness'.[15] This study undertakes to analyse the way character consciousness is explored especially in the last three novels.

A general but important characteristic which I attempt to examine in Meredith's exploitation of realism is his conviction that the world of his fiction is not essentially knowable. I hope to demonstrate that a fuller appreciation of Meredith's world of fiction can be obtained through the attempt to explore the complexity of character and not through the search, indulged in by contemporary reviewers and modern critics, for a shared moral scheme linking the community and the 'old stable ego of the character'.[16]

2 *The Ordeal of Richard Feverel*: the Shaping Experience

The *Ordeal* is the story of Meredith the artist as a man of ordeal. While writing it, Meredith himself was undergoing the experience of desertion by his first wife, Mary Ellen Nicholls, who had eloped with the painter Henry Wallis late in 1858, and left Meredith with their five year old son, Arthur. The situation is described by Lionel Stevenson in his biography of Meredith: 'Their elopement marked the end of a year of torment for Meredith. First the gradual conviction that his wife loved someone else, then the grim farce of keeping up a public appearance of amity between them, next the shame and bitterness of the decision over the baby's paternity [the son born to Mary on 18 April], and finally the open disgrace of her flight—all these combined to inflict upon him an incalculable shock.'[1]

Meredith's attitude towards his ordeal was characterised by reticence. His state of mind at the time is alluded to in a letter to his friend Eyre Crowe (28 April 1858): 'How shall I amuse my Crowe? If I speak much, old fellow, I shall get to speaking of myself, and that is not a cheerful theme . . . .' The letter concludes: 'If you are to stay from us any time, pray, write to me again. Don't be shocked at my dull reply. I'll get more news next time. I am ill, overworked, vexed. I'll do better by degrees. Take the good intent just now.' (1, 34–5)

Meredith's reticence over the actual ordeal provided him with the mask to present the fictional ordeal. This mask or what may, perhaps, be described as the aesthetic or the rational distance should, I think, stand at the core of any discussion which sets out to clarify or reassess the purpose of the book.

Meredith, then, approached *The Ordeal* with the impulse to write about his personal experience and, at the same time, the need to separate himself from its subject matter. The result is a state of dichotomy in which Meredith found himself caught in what T. S. Eliot calls *depersonalisation* where 'the more perfect the artist, the more completely separate in him will be the man who suffers and the mind which creates; the more perfectly will the mind digest and transmute the passions which are its material.'[2] Out of this state of conflict comes the vitality of the book as manifested in the main character, Sir Austin.

Like his creator, Sir Austin has an ordeal to cope with and a counter-ordeal in which he takes refuge (in Meredith it is the actual process of writing itself). For him the ordeal is irrational—something like a shock whose effect can never be undone. Its effect, however, drives him not to surrender, but into devising a way of surviving it. In this conflict Sir Austin tries to discover, rather than recover from, his ordeal. The System he devises for the education of his son is designed as a rational counter to the irrational effect of the ordeal. It is a kind of objectification of his feeling.

Meredith's achievement in *The Ordeal* can, I think, be demonstrated by examining the relationship between Sir Austin and his System, and, at the same time, between Sir Austin and the main agents of the System, namely, Adrian and Lady Blandish. In this relationship lies the distance between 'the man who suffers and the mind which creates'.

Sir Austin's System is originally more of a rationale for the contemplation of a father's situation than a rational device for the education of a son. To survive the private ordeal rationally, Sir Austin turns to public affairs in the hope of suspending, if not countering, the strain of the situation.

The desire in Sir Austin to rationalise is a by-product of his experience of the ordeal. In the meantime rationalisation, as conceived of by Sir Austin, is to be directed not towards the experience itself, but rather towards achieving a stable perspective on it. Hence Sir Austin's concern with a perspective for the history of his son and with the public issues of education. It is here, I think, that Sir Austin demonstrates that he is not a mere egoist or even a utilitarian egoist but rather an egoist who is conscious of his egoism and who, at the same time, tries to dissociate himself from his egoism so as to view his situation objectively.[3]

The *Ordeal* recalls Lytton's *The Caxtons* (1849) and *My Novel* (1853) where the intellectual background of the time is used so as to produce a sentimental account of popular ideas of education. It is even more reminiscent of Novalis's story *The Blue Flower* in which Novalis tries the merit of the recorded thoughts of men by exposing them to the test of an ordeal.

The description of Richard's early education suggests that the System was designed to follow nature. Similar ideas had been made popular on the continent by writers such as Rousseau, Pestalozzi and Froebel, while in England, Herbert Spencer had written three extensive articles describing 'sequential' education.[4]

Spencer emphasises the role of nature in education, contrasting its efficacy with that of human intervention: 'The truly instructive and salutary consequences are not those inflicted by parents when they take upon themselves to be Nature's proxies; but they are those inflicted by Nature herself.'[5] In *The Ordeal* various allusions are made to the effect that the System violates nature. Adrian warns Sir Austin that 'Nature never forgives', and 'The Pilgrim's Scrip' urges us to remember 'that Nature, though heathenish, reaches at her best to the footstool of the Highest. She is not all dust, but a living portion of the spheres. In aspiration it is our error to despise her, forgetting that through Nature only can we ascend.' (XXVI, 177) This recalls Spencer's conception of Nature as a strict accountant.[6]

Another aspect of the public debate on education is seen in the tension between theory and practice, or in the application of the ideal to get pragmatic results. Auguste Comte, for example, who was already established on the continent and whose philosophy was gradually becoming popular in England, wrote that one important effect of Positive Philosophy 'will be to regenerate education'. 'The best minds are agreed that our European education, still essentially theological, metaphysical, and literary, must be superseded by a Positive training comfortable to our time and needs.'[7] William Whewell similarly remarked that 'Art is the application of Science to the purpose of practical life.'[8]

Sir Austin was originally a 'Scientific Humanist', believing in the perfectibility of man: 'He had been noble Love to the one, and to the other perfect Friendship. He had bid them be brother and sister, whom he loved, and live a Golden Age with him at Raynham. In fact, he had been prodigal of the excellencies of his nature, which it is not good to be, and, like Timon, he became bankrupt, and fell upon bitterness.' (II, 14) His belief in a 'Golden Age' is the clue to the origin of the ordeal. Having failed to realise this belief with his friend and wife, he turns to his son, with a plan to conduct another test of the hypothesis of the perfectibility of man:

> The gist of the System set forth: That a Golden Age, or something near it, might yet be established on our sphere, when fathers accepted their solemn responsibility, and studied human nature with a Scientific eye, knowing what a high Science it is, to live: and that, by hedging round the Youth from corruptness, and at the same time promoting his animal health, by helping him to grow, as he would, like a Tree of Eden; by advancing him to a certain moral fortitude ere the Apple-Disease was spontaneously developed, there would be seen something approaching to a perfect Man, as the Baronet trusted to make this one Son of his, after a receipt of his own. (1, 9)

Sir Austin's intention to prevent Richard's union with any woman until the time deemed appropriate by the System is basically motivated by a rational design intended to provide the 'Scientific Humanist' with the opportunity to extend his notions of the moral being of man. As he believes in the 'rightness' of this intervention he simultaneously tends to control Richard's moral activity by his own moral ideas.

In his attempt to enforce moral laws or what Whewell describes as 'the antithesis in morals' here, Sir Austin again reflects a current preoccupation of the time. Whewell supposes that man, being an agent in determining events of the external world (natural world) acquires ability to determine the action of man (moral world), and to set laws for them. He refers to the way man makes facts out of his ideas: 'The Moral Acts without are the results of Moral Ideas within.' He remarks that 'what he [man] thinks of as wrong, he tries to prevent; what he deems right he attempts to realise'. Whewell classifies man's history according to the promotion or violation of moral ideas. The extension of moral ideas into the region of facts, he sees, expresses 'the history of man as man'; while 'the history of man as brute' is expressed by his acts of desire and by facts which have no moral character. He identifies the constant progress of humanity with the realisation of moral ideas, whether in the natural or moral world. He sees positivism as the extension of human knowledge to human action.[9]

Positivist philosophy, coupled with the theory of evolution, seemed to provide a refuge from emotional and intellectual dilemmas. It acted as a substitute for a lost belief or tradition, and at the same time rationalised the loss in the name of progress. Spencer, for example, found in the idea of natural cause and effect a substitute for religious faith. Sir Austin, similarly, finds in his system hope for the future of his son just as he finds consolation in the rationalisation of his own loss. This is revealed in the narrative tempo, which often moves forward into the history of the son and occasionally backward to the history of the father. It is further seen in Chapter xxv where 'Richard is summoned to town to hear a sermon'. The main theme of the sermon is women and the ordeal they are capable of inflicting on men. Sir Austin shows an ability to generalise intellectually, not from abstract thought but from personal experience.[10] As he refers to the episode of the ordeal he says:

> 'You had, in your infancy, a great loss.' Father and son coloured simultaneously. 'To make that good to you, I chose to isolate myself from the world, and devote myself entirely to your welfare; and I think it is not vanity that tells me now, that the son I have reared is one of the most hopeful of God's creatures. But for that very reason, you are open to be tempted the most, and to sink the deepest. It was the First of the Angels who made the road to Hell.'
>   He paused again. Richard fingered at his watch.
>   'In our House, my son, there is peculiar blood. We go to wreck very easily. It sounds like superstition,—I cannot but think we are tried as most men are not. I see it in us all.'

He then turns to the subject of women:

> 'It is when you encounter them that you are thoroughly on trial. It is when you know them that Life is either a mockery to you, or, as some find it, a gift of blessedness. They are our Ordeal. Love of any human object is the soul's Ordeal; and they are ours, loving them, or not.' (xxv, 165)

The integration of matters of public concern with Sir Austin's private ordeal adds vitality to his character and widens the scope for its portrayal. In Lukacs's terms, it enables Meredith to present the totality of Sir Austin's character with 'the intellectual physiognomy'.[11]

The distance, originally provided by the System, is enacted by

Adrian, who is appointed by Sir Austin as one guardian for Richard's upbringing. For Sir Austin, Adrian is a kind of secret sharer. In practical terms he does what Sir Austin wishes that he himself could do.

The fact that Adrian survives his own ordeal with good humour makes him admirable to Sir Austin, who views him, consciously or unconsciously, as an external actualisation of his own potential. Adrian pushes the distance between Sir Austin and the System to the extreme. The attitude Adrian adopts towards his ordeal would be ideal for Sir Austin. It is the secret but ideal self lurking in the background of Sir Austin's mind.

Meredith's identification with the character of Sir Austin, resulting in the confusion of aesthetic distance between narrator and character, is offset by the detachment of Adrian Harley.[12] The comic nature of this character, standing as it does between the narrator and Sir Austin, helps to establish a distance from the ordeal.

Like all the residents of the Abbey, Adrian has had his own ordeal, for his father, 'Mr Justice Harley, died in his promising son's College term, bequeathing him nothing but his legal complexion, and Adrian became stipendiary officer in his Uncle's household'. (IV, 25) The narrative voice records a belief, held by Mrs Doria and considered by the author to be 'merely right', that Adrian had no heart. 'A singular mishap (at his birth, possibly, or before it) had unseated that organ, and shaken it down to his stomach, where it was a much lighter, nay, an inspiring, weight, and encouraged him merrily onward.' (IV, 25)

Adrian's rationalisation of the ordeal of life consists in avoiding any serious thinking and feeling; instead he indulges himself in sensual pleasures:

Adrian was an Epicurean: one whom Epicurus would have scourged out of his Garden, certainly: an Epicurean of our modern notions. To satisfy his appetites without rashly staking his character, was the Wise Youth's problem for life. He had no intimates save Gibbon and Horace, and the society of these fine aristocrats of literature helped him to accept humanity as it had been, and was; a Supreme Ironic Procession, with Laughter of Gods in the background. Why not Laughter of Mortals also? Adrian had his laugh in his comfortable corner. He possessed peculiar attributes of a Heathen God. (IV, 24)

Meredith emphasises Adrian's sensuality: 'A fat Wise Youth, digesting well: charming after dinner, with men, or with women: soft, dimpled, succulent-looking as a sucking-pig: delightfully sarcastic: perhaps a little too unscrupulous in his moral tone, but that his moral reputation belied him, and it must be set down to generosity of disposition'. (IV, 25) The narrator comments (apparently with favour) on Adrian's attitude as he views it in correspondence with the morality of the world: 'Nature and he attempted no other concealment than the ordinary mask men wear. And yet the world would proclaim him moral, as well as wise, and the pleasing converse everyway of his disgraced cousin, Austin'. (IV, 24)

Adrian is a 'fellow-actor' to the System for 'The Wise Youth spread out his mind to it like a piece of blank paper.' He laughs at Sir Austin: ' "A monomaniac at large, watching over sane people in slumber!" thinks Adrian Harley, as he hears Sir Austin's footfall, and truly that was a strange object to see, [but one not so strange in his service]' (VII, 48; the bracketed section is deleted in revision). Adrian's laughter is not generated by the Comic Spirit or guided by its moral power. It is laughter of indifference.

Adrian is chosen by Sir Austin to superintend Richard's education because of his positive attitude to the ordeal of life. Sir Austin was impressed by Adrian's comment on Austin Wentworth's ordeal: 'Adrian Harley, who had no views of his own on the subject, except that it was absurd when you were in the mud to plunge in deeper instead of jumping out, cleverly interpreted his Chief's, and delighted him with swelling periods.' (IV, 23) Following this, they had a conference together 'and from that time Adrian became a fixture in the Abbey'.

Sir Austin enjoys Adrian's comedy. On the occasion of the apparition of Mrs Malediction, for example, 'he could laugh on hearing Adrian, in reminiscence of the ill luck of one of the family members at its first manifestation, call the uneasy spirit, Algernon's Leg'. (XV, 88) And when Lady Blandish says to Sir Austin that Richard 'seems to care for nothing, not even for the beauty of the day,' he adds: 'Or Adrian's jokes'. (XXIX, 203)

However the comedy of Adrian remains limited in its effect on Sir Austin, and its limitation is fixed from the beginning and not, as it is often considered, towards the last quarter of the book.[13] In Adrian Sir Austin views the ideal image of himself in opposition to the actual self. At times of difficulty Sir Austin yearns for Adrian's, instead of Lady Blandish's, company (xxxvii, 288), but the division between him and Adrian remains as that between theory and practice.

Adrian helps Meredith to define the conflict between the rational and the irrational in Sir Austin's approach to the ordeal. No other character around Sir Austin helps towards this end because of their attachment to their own ordeals as well as to that of Sir Austin and his son.

The contrast between Adrian's attitude and that of all other characters is demonstrated in the rick-burning incident which Adrian views with total indifference: ' "Boys are like monkeys," remarked Adrian, at the close of his explosions, "the gravest actors of farcical nonsense that the world possesses. May I never be where there are no boys! A couple of boys left to themselves will furnish richer fun than any troop of trained comedians. No: no Art arrives at the artlessness of Nature in matters of Comedy . . ." '. (ix, 59) Later in the scene the dialogue between Adrian and Austin Wentworth reveals that all partners involved, except Adrian, consider it a major crisis of the System:

> Adrian always made a point of feeding the fretful beast, Impatience, with pleasantries; a not congenial diet; and Austin, the most patient of human beings, began to lose his self-control.
>
> 'You talk as if Time belonged to you, Adrian. We have but a few hours left us. Work first, and joke afterwards. The boy's fate is being decided now.'
>
> 'So is everybody's, my dear Austin!' yawned the Epicurean.
>
> 'Yes, but this boy is at present under our guardianship: under yours especially.'
>
> 'Not yet! not yet!' Adrian interjected languidly. 'No getting into scrapes when I have him. The leash, young hound! The collar, young colt! I'm perfectly irresponsible at present.'
>
> 'You may have something different to deal with, when you are responsible, if you think that.'
>
> 'I take my young Prince as I find him, coz: a Julian, or a Caracalla: a Constantine, or a Nero. Then if he will play the fiddle to a conflagration, he shall play it well: if he must be a disputatious apostate, at any rate, he shall understand logic and men, and have the habit of saying his prayers.'
>
> 'Then you leave me to act alone?' said Austin, rising.
>
> 'Without a single curb!' Adrian gesticulated an acquiesced

withdrawal. 'I'm sure you would not, still more certain you cannot, do harm. And be mindful of my prophetic words: Whatever's done, Old Blaize will have to be bought off. There's the affair settled at once. I suppose I must go to the Chief to-night, and settle it myself. We can't see this poor devil condemned, though it's nonsense to talk of a boy being the prime instigator.' (IX, 61)

Dealing with the same incident, Sir Austin, Austin Wentworth, Algernon, and Richard—all, in fact, except Adrian—go to Farmer Blaize to settle the matter. Adrian is 'so persuasive and aphoristic' in his objection to the scheme, but Sir Austin has a better aphorism of his own to confute him with.

'Expediency is man's wisdom, Adrian Harley. Doing Right is God's.'
Adrian curbed his desire to ask Sir Austin whether an attempt to counteract the just working of the Law, was Doing Right. The direct application of an Aphorism was unpopular at Raynham. (XVII, 80)

The contrast between Adrian and Lady Blandish is similarly displayed, as in the dialogue between the two at Lobourne:

'Quite a lover's night,' said Lady Blandish.
'And I, who have none to love—pity me!' The Wise Youth attempted a sigh. (XXIV, 152)

Throughout the book the comedy of Adrian remains free from the moral discipline of Meredith's developed comedy. It continues to be directed towards no end beyond exciting laughter out of the serious involvement of other characters. From the scene between Richard and Hippias, Adrian, for example, 'got so much fun out of the notion of these two journeying together, and the mishaps that might occur to them, that he esteemed it almost a personal insult for his hearers not to laugh'. (XXIX, 203) At the beginning of Chapter XLV Adrian welcomes Austin Wentworth's return with laughter at his serious involvement in current politics.

Apart from its main relevance to the central character in the book the comedy of Adrian reflects a contemporary ethical concern in the sense that it guards the book against the negative reaction anticipated from the reading public in respect to the morbidity of the ordeal. A few years before the appearance of the book *The Westminster Review*, for example, had warned novelists against painful themes in fiction. Reviewing *Florence Templer*, an autobiography, and *The Wedding Guests; or the Happiness of Life* by Mary C. Hume, the review criticised the writers for presenting painful themes in fiction: 'If life in the present is to be portrayed, some hard things must needs obtrude. The province of Art is to subordinate and soften them down. There are few subjects not legitimate to the novelist, but as we are happily constituted to shun and detest the sight of evil, it should be the novelist's care not to give what is painful undue prominence and especially not to strike a doubtful chord in the mind.'[14] Meredith himself admits, in a letter, that he is inclined to present morbidity in his fiction but makes a conscious effort to repress it. (I, 322–3) Mrs Oliphant similarly objects to the presentation of painful subjects in fiction and considers it futile to deal with subjects which achieve no satisfactory result. In her study G. L. Griest explains this tendency, which is basically ethical, as partly reflecting 'the general optimism' and partly 'the result of the growing realisation of the educational possibilities of fiction'.[15]

Comedy does not, however, overcome the pain of the ordeal. Sir Austin's oscillation between Adrian and Lady Blandish, and the different ways in which each helps him to view the ordeal, indicate Meredith's oscillation between the impulse to repress and the impulse to reveal his sympathy with the subject of the ordeal. Although the effect of comedy diminishes towards the end of the book as Lady Blandish's influence increases, no conflict is developed between the two, thus the efficacy of comedy is never tested.

Lady Blandish provides variety of tone as well as of distance. She is closer to the ordeal of father and son than any of the inmates of the Abbey. Her intimacy with Sir Austin, like Richard's union with Lucy, suggests the failure of the System from the start, because the author of 'The Pilgrim's Scrip' is known for a perversity of view regarding women. This is ironically demonstrated in the incident of the bonnet where Richard, during a match, catches a glimpse of his father flirting with Lady Blandish. (XV, 94) The incident provokes Richard's curiosity about the two sexes at a time when the System demands that he should be protected from such incidents.

Lady Blandish is presumably an advocate of the System, but unlike those women advocates such as Doria Austin and Mrs Grandison who are reduced to tools used by the System, she is individualised by the flexibility of her attitude. Her involvement in the System does not curb her personal feelings, and her emotional attitude to Sir Austin provokes a response as seen in the dialogue between the two (XVI, 101–4), where the variety of tone reveals gaiety, earnestness and comic spirit.

'Oh!' said Lady Blandish to Sir Austin, 'if men could give their hands to women unsoiled—how different would many a marriage be! She will be a happy girl who calls Richard husband.'

'Happy indeed!' was the Baronet's caustic ejaculation. 'But where shall I meet one equal to him, and his match?'

'I was innocent when I was a girl,' said the lady.

Sir Austin bowed a reserved opinion.

'Do you think no girls innocent?'

Sir Austin gallantly thought them all so.

'No, that you know they are not,' said the lady, stamping. 'But they are more innocent than boys, I am sure.'

'Because of their Education, Madam. You see now what a youth can be. Perhaps, when my System is published, or rather—to speak more humbly—when it is practised, the balance may be restored, and we shall have virtuous young men.'

'It's too late for poor me to hope for a husband from one of them,' said the lady, pouting and laughing.

'It is never too late for Beauty to waken Love,' returned the Baronet, and they trifled a little. They were approaching Daphne's Bower, which they entered, and sat there to taste the coolness of a descending Midsummer day.

The Baronet seemed in a humour for dignified fooling; the lady for serious converse.

Lady Blandish then talks about her knightly dreams but in a serious manner, and Sir Austin's response is comic. In one of her replies she says: 'Ah! you know men, but not women.' The tone continues to fluctuate until Sir Austin exclaims 'Good God! . . . women have much to bear.' The narrative voice comments, 'Here the couple changed characters. The lady became gay as the Baronet grew earnest.' The dialogue proceeds and ends with Lady Blandish's offer (accepted with appreciation by Sir Austin) to be the adoptive mother of Richard. 'Call him ours, Madam,' he 'most graciously appended.' The situation implies that the ordeal is not solely in the betrayal of husband but also in the desertion of son.

Lady Blandish, like Adrian, is not a character who is able to alleviate the ordeal. Her sympathetic response provides the opportunity for Sir Austin to expose his dilemma and to disclose his personal thoughts and feelings about the System and what lies behind it. The communication between the two is controlled by the degree of frankness Sir Austin offers, and, as he is uncertain about his attitude, Lady Blandish spontaneously controls her response. This explains the alternation of tone and the confusing effect which the wooing scene produces. To mitigate confusion the narrator refers to both partners as sentimentalists.

In 'Nursing the Devil' Sir Austin speaks to Lady Blandish as a disillusioned practitioner rather than a designer of the System: 'You see, Emmeline, it is useless to base any System on a human being'. (XXXVII, 284) In his state of disillusionment Sir Austin envisages his ordeal in general terms, but his generalisation always suggests his specific personal ordeal: ' "You know, Emmeline," he added, "I believe very little in the fortune, or misfortune, to which men attribute their successes and reverses. They are useful impersonations to novelists; but my opinion is sufficiently high of flesh and blood to believe that we make our own history without intervention. Accidents?—Terrible misfortunes?—What are they?—Good night" '. (XXXVII, 285)

The point under discussion is that of cause and effect in human action. Sir Austin tries to convey to Lady Blandish his conclusion that one's ordeal is determined by one's own action rather than by any external factor. When Lady Blandish sensibly asks Sir Austin to take into consideration his son's pride, sensitiveness and his great wild nature, he replies:

'That I should save him, or any one, from consequences, is asking more than the order of things will allow to you, Emmeline, and is not in the disposition of this world. I cannot. Consequences are the natural offspring of acts. My child, you are talking sentiment, which is the distraction of our modern age in everything—a phantasmal vapour distorting the image of the life we live. You ask me to give him a golden age in spite of himself. All that could be done, by keeping him in the paths of Virtue and Truth, I did. He is become a man, and as a man he must reap his own sowing.' (XXXVII, 290)

The dialogue here makes a contrast which is parallel to the previous one. It marks a considerable change in Sir Austin as he comes to distrust the role of man as Providence—a role he thinks Lady Blandish prompts him to adopt. He drifts to the extreme of believing that even his love for his son might demand a further intervention in Richard's future education, and a continuation of the System which he now realises to be a failure. Sir Austin consequently accepts a new system of independence for Richard: a negation of his own System.

Lady Blandish cannot fully grasp the metaphysics of the ordeal of father and son as rationalised by Sir Austin. She simply thinks that the father's forgiveness (his love) would bring their ordeal to an end, but the fact that Sir Austin's forgiveness (granted later on) proves to be useless in preventing the ordeal shows that Lady Blandish is oversimplifying the situation. In this sense Lady Blandish's pleading and previous wooing can be considered, in comparison with Adrian's realistic attitude, sentimental.

There is less mutual response in this encounter between Lady Blandish and Sir Austin because there is less direct expression of feelings. The gap in communication between the two is implied in Lady Blandish's failure to understand Sir Austin's thought as he generalises his specific personal grief.

It is further suggested by the allusion to the bafflement of Lady Blandish, and Sir Austin's longing for Adrian's company. Their failure to communicate seems to impose silence on Sir Austin and to invite Lady Blandish to share his ideas about the situation: 'You would console me, Emmeline, with the prospect that, if he ruins himself, he spares the world of young women. Yes, that is something! that is something!' (xxxvii, 290)

However the link between the two remains strong; for though Sir Austin realises that Lady Blandish finds his reasoning alien, he feels that she is close to his heart as the conclusion of the scene reveals: '"God's rarest blessing is, after all, a good woman! My Emmeline bears her sleepless night well. She does not shame the day." He gazed down on her with a fondling tenderness'. (xxxvii, 291) This suggests that Sir Austin needed Lady Blandish's sympathy in the same way as he needed Adrian's detachment so as to suspend rather than to put an end to his ordeal.

However the state of suspense in the narrative has, at one point or another, to be disrupted when the artistic demand of ending is needed. For Meredith it was not an easy task because it meant a disruption in the vital interplay of the two impulses he had manager to hold in balance, and his way out of the dilemma was the shift of emphasis from the immanent catastrophe of father to the imminent tragedy of son. Hence the gradual withdrawal of the father from the life of his son as the narrative draws to an end. In Frank Kermode's term the ending may be described as a kind of *apocalypse* in which Richard, for example, is given 'the freedom' to choose and so to alter the structure, the relations of beginning, middle and end.[16]

In 'The Last Scene' Sir Austin realises that his System was, 'beyond a certain point,' presumptuous, and an offending son is forgiven. The narrative voice comments: 'False to his son it could not be said that he had been: false to his System he was. Others saw it plainly, but he had to learn his lesson by-and-by' (XLVIII, 417). 'The Last Scene' completes the partial disillusionment; in 'Nursing the Devil' Sir Austin discredits the System only in practice, and in 'The Last Scene' the System is discredited even in principle. This is the last stage of the interplay of theory and practice.

The book could have ended happily here, with the end of the ordeal. The tragic ending, undoubtedly painful, has its own artistic justification, despite the fact that its tragic sense has never been fully allowed by critics.

A close examination of the ending shows that tragedy is not inconsistent with the total design of the book, for until the end the two impulses remain irreconcilable.

One may assume that Meredith envisaged two conclusions of the book as the only solution for his state of oscillation, and this, I think, is what explains the succession of happy reconciliation and tragic ending. Here Meredith's letter to Lucas can be taken as an expression of his uncertainty in viewing the System as alternately a success and a failure. Robert Sencourt perceptively comments that Meredith's difficulty was 'that he could neither rid himself of the past, nor yet build on it'.[17] On one occasion Meredith said to Clodd: 'I keep on the causeway between the bogs of optimism and pessimism'.[18]

In aesthetic terms a happy ending would, perhaps, have suggested to Meredith a submission to 'an audience impatient for blood and glory'—two aspects of sensational fiction against which he reacted violently. At the same time a happy reconciliation would lead to the conclusion that the purpose of the book was a moral triumph. With the tragic ending, then, Meredith finds a solution for a technical problem.

The tragedy was not 'a sharp snap or a crash', as Justin

McCarthy remarked.[19] Its origin can be traced in the last third of
the book where the emphasis shifts from the father's concern with
the education of his son to the son's concern with his own career.
After Chapter xxxvii Sir Austin's action is subordinated to
Richard's romanticism—out of which comes the nemesis of tragedy.
Without Sir Austin's vigilance, the comedy of Adrian, and Lady
Blandish's sympathy, the true nature of the ordeal—its tragedy—
remains a matter of actuality. The overt side gives way to the inner
meaning of the book. The tragedy begins to shape itself as Richard
begins to play his own 'providence'. Romanticism then replaces the
previous overt design. The two designs are essentially different in
function; for while the first suspends the tragedy, the second
gradually leads to it.

Richard is a knight-errant. This is particularly displayed in his
connection with female characters. He tries hard to rescue Clare
from the loveless marriage arranged for her. In a hopeless adventure
he attempts to rescue his mother. However the narrative voice
intervenes to guard against taking Richard lightly: 'Hero as he was,'
Meredith says, 'a youth, open to the insane promptings of hot blood,
he was not a fool'. (xli, 336) With Mrs Mount, Richard is a
champion who works out a scheme for saving fallen women. His
connection with Lady Judith has similar motivation. He discusses
with her a joint plan to reform the world. They review social and
political affairs.

Romanticism can be defined here as a state of illusion, and its
expression is in knight-errant behaviour. Lady Judith tries to help
Richard become dissatisfied with his situation. 'Was I not there to
applaud you? I only think such energies should be turned into some
definitely useful channel. But you must not go into the Army'.
(xxxviii, 302)[20] She advises Richard not to be too romantic, and
envisages in him a knight-errant, but her efforts do not succeed, and
Richard continues to live with the 'images of airy towers hung
around'. Later in the book Richard is described contemplating the
rank he would take in the liberating army. (xlvi, 402) Meredith
again, forewarns the reader against taking Richard's illusion as a
'laughing matter', thus foreshadowing the tragedy.[21]

At this stage Sir Austin views the tragedy of the ordeal in Richard
in the same way that he earlier viewed the differing attitudes of
Adrian and Lady Blandish towards the ordeal. The disillusioned
father helplessly watches the tragic illusion of the son in Chapter
xxxvii. He perceives Richard's illusion as a parallel to his own just

before the ordeal. Sir Austin's insight comes from his disillusion with his own youth. The discrepancy between the disillusioned father and the never-disillusioned son in the last part of the book foretells in its undertones a forthcoming tragedy. The purpose of the book acquires more clarity towards the end because of the distance between the mature narrator and the immature youth. Here Sir Austin can detach himself from the ordeal and see it more clearly than before.

Tragedy in *The Ordeal* arises, then, from Richard's inability to rise above his illusion, as the last words of the book suggest. 'Have you noticed the expression in the eyes of blind men? That is just how Richard looks, as he lies there silent in his bed—striving to image her [Lucy] on his brain' XLIX, 432). With some modification of the situation the same words could have been said by Meredith on the occasion of Arthur's death in 1888, which for Meredith was, perhaps, the last act of the ordeal he actually witnessed.

It can be argued that the artistic flaw in *The Ordeal* is essentially related to the lack of a positive power to help Richard come to terms with the reconciliation at the Abbey and prevent him from drifting to a fatal knight-errantry. Arnold Kettle, for example, comments: 'All the positive forces of the novel depend on an objective definition, within the terms of art, of Richard's and Lucy's romantic love. But this never comes. The relationship is never "placed" '.[22] It is true that Richard's love for Lucy remains undefined in the sense that it does not provide him with a counterpower against an ineffectual idealism. However a positive definition of love in this sense would appear out of proportion in a book originally motivated by a negative attitude to the ordeal, as described in Meredith's letter to his friend Crowe. By the time *The Ordeal* was coming to an end the tragedy of the ordeal was perhaps still 'congruent to all that was real to him'.[23] For an objective definition of the positive forces of romantic love we have to turn to *Harry Richmond* where one impulse is reconciled to the other as Harry gradually evolves out of his state of illusion.

3 The Adventures of Harry Richmond: the Crowning Experience

This is Meredith's second exploration of the history of father and son, and Meredith calls it (significantly) the 'Adventures of Father and Son'. It is by no means the same history whose centre he personally was when it actually happened. *Harry Richmond* is comparatively remote in its time and place, and this obviously helped Meredith to gain control over this history. In this attempt Meredith not only managed to carry with him the personal intensity of the subject which he seems to have cherished over the years but also succeeded in objectifying its power.

Like many English novelists of his time Meredith had the desire 'to examine *impersonally* the experience of growing up' in the middle of the nineteenth century through the *Bildungsroman*, the formal model of which is *Wilhelm Meister* (See Appendixes I and II). For Meredith the *Bildungsroman* was one solution concerning the rational distance between fiction and reality where the form justifies the content.

There is no direct reference to *Wilhelm Meister* in *Harry Richmond*, but the allusions available suggest that Meredith was particularly fond of *Wilhelm Meister* as well as an admirer of Goethe.[1] The Professor, opening discussion with Harry about his scheme of life, refers to 'Shakespeare's book; or Göthe's'. (xxix, 311) Again, Harry, waiting to meet Ottilia, 'was humming the burden of Göthe's Zigeunerlied, a favourite one with [him] whenever [he] had too much to think of, or nothing'. (xxxv, 382) A third allusion occurs when the Countess Szezedy says to Harry, 'So, . . . you are to marry the romantic head, the Princess Ottilia of Eppenwelzen! I know her well. I have met her in Vienna. Schöne Seele, and bas bleu! It's just those that are won with a duel . . .'. (xxxix, 439)

In general terms various aspects of plot and character in *Harry*

Richmond can be identified with those of *Wilhelm Meister*. Both novels are mainly concerned with the development of the hero through self-cultivation. This development is enacted by two stages: the early stage where the mind of the boy is receptive and enchanted by the wonders of the external world, and the later stage where the mind of the adult faces a difficult moral choice which involves self-realisation as well as self-justification. The theme of father and son is a main pattern in the two novels, and the death of the fathers leaves the sons free but undecided, and it is here where the shaping conflict of their maturity is intensified.

Plot and character structure in *Harry Richmond* remain, however, far less complicated than in *Wilhelm Meister*. The wide range of sensational events which Goethe and the reading public of his time favoured has no parallel in *Harry Richmond*. Wilhelm's emotional involvement, for example, is more complicated and entangled than Harry's. Wilhelm was captured by Mignon, when he proposed to Theresa and was infatuated with Natalie. Harry's dilemma, on the other hand, is limited to the choice between Janet and Ottilia.

In the same way that Goethe's *Wilhelm Meister* provided Meredith with the general characteristics of the *Bildungsroman*, Dickens's *David Copperfield* and *Great Expectations* seemed to draw his attention to the specific application of the genre itself. One may even claim that Meredith borrowed the title of his novel from what was briefly stated on the cover of each instalment of *David Copperfield*: 'The Personal History, Adventures, Experience, and Observation of David Copperfield.'

The way the boyhood mind of Harry perceives things is very reminiscent of that of David's, for both react to the external world with wonder and spontaneity. Both are enchanted by the same book of romance: *The Arabian Nights*. Their pictures come to us through the fresh vision of the boy narrator. One feels as if the early part of the two novels was written by a boy, and one may not feel the same about Wilhelm whose picture is, by comparison presented mostly through the eyes of the mature boy narrator.

However, the adult David is the kind of adult who wishes to remain a boy (and this does not apply to the adult Harry). When Dickens was writing *Great Expectations* he seemed to have realised in retrospect the dominant effect of the picture of boyhood even in the adult David. Dickens's letter to Forster is suggestive of this effect: 'The book will be written in the first person throughout, and during these first three weekly numbers you will find the hero to be a boy-child, like David. Then he will be an apprentice.'[2] Meredith's correspondence (to be discussed later) concerning the evolving personality and 'the gradual changes in the growing Harry', expresses his concern for the apprentice, Harry, in a similar manner to that of Dickens in his letter to Forster in which he expresses his own ideas for the apprentice, Pip. The result of this apprenticeship is the inevitability of change which comes out of suffering, and this is common ground shared by the three novels, *Wilhelm Meister*, *Great Expectations* and *Harry Richmond*.

In his discussion of *Harry Richmond* Robert Sencourt points (not favourably, though) to what may be taken as the emergence of some artistic control in Meredith over his art; and it escapes his attention, I think, that his observation is the key to the appreciation of the novel. It is true, as he remarks, that *Harry Richmond* 'has neither the poetic force and energy of *Vittoria*, nor the delightful comedy of *Evan Harrington*, nor the tragic ardour and power of *The Ordeal*.'[3] But the novel was designed to present a different picture of adventures, comedy, and the father–son relationship. In the course of Meredith's artistic development *Harry Richmond* is as much of an innovation for him as *Great Expectations* was for Dickens.

One kind of innovation is carried out through the picture of the mind of the young narrator. The romance of Riversley, the lodgings and school where Harry finds himself placed by his father, the gypsy world, Captain Welsh and his Priscilla—all come to us through the fresh vision of the boy narrator. The same is true of the response of Pip to his surroundings, the convict and the marshes, Joe and the country life, and Miss Havisham and Satis House.

Misrepresentation of the purpose of each novel begins if one overlooks the interplay between the mind of the narrator and the external world of his surroundings. This is how contemporary reviewers were led to view romance as a world of exciting incidents recounted by a mature narrator. In fact, in these two novels, romance is generated by the response of the child or the adolescent to his world and marks one stage in the development towards full adulthood.

The other aspect of innovation, which is complementary in nature to the previous one, emerges from the picture of the mature narrator. This implies adaptation in the feelings of the narrator as he moves towards maturity. The result is the transformation of the external world through a different consciousness. It is not, then, that the world described is disrupted after a certain point in the narrative of *Harry Richmond* and *Great Expectations*; Squire Beltham's world, Roy's, Captain Welsh's, and the gypsy's—are in themselves unchanged. So are Magwitch's, Joe's, and Miss Havisham's.

However, when it comes to the resolution of the plot, each novelist follows a different turn. Goethe concludes his novel with a kind of fairy-tale happy ending. For Dickens such an ending was not possible, as he was inclined to believe that suffering was permanently damaging in the sense that a return to spontaneity and happiness was thus rendered impossible. The ending (as it stands) of *Great Expectations* suggests that suffering may be alleviated but not healed altogether. The original ending further suggests that suffering cannot be obliterated and consequently replaced by happiness. This notion of suffering has the kind of psychological realism which would presumably be lacking in a straightforward happy ending.

In resolving the plot of *Harry Richmond* Meredith fluctuates between a Goethean and Dickensian ending, a dilemma clearly demonstrated by the revisions he makes towards the end of the book. At one time Meredith contemplated, or so it would seem, a conclusion without a happy ending, with Janet left unchanged by suffering and unable to accept union with Harry, but Meredith was eventually tempted to adopt the Goethean fairy-tale ending rather than the Dickensian sorrowful one. This may be justified on the ground that suffering in *Harry Richmond* is not as intense as it is in *Great Expectations*, and is comparatively less damaging.

Other parallels can be established between *Great Expectations* and *Harry Richmond*. The fairy-tale pattern out of which Pip and Harry gradually emerge is one such. Both have the inclination to explore the world outside their provincial environment. Harry is instructed by his father that his fortune lies in gaining Ottilia; in a similar manner Pip is instructed by his sister and Pumblechook of what Miss Havisham 'would do with me and for me'.

A most striking parallel is, however, that of the beating of Harry by the gypsies on the one hand, and on the other, the murderous assault on Pip by Orlick. In both the situation is not simple melodrama. The Pip–Orlick relationship has mystery and romance but without any explicit moral definition. Orlick commits the assault simply because he is Orlick. In the meantime, we do not know (at least it is not explicit in the text) whether Pip accepts the incident simply because it happens or because he thinks it should happen.

Pip, we know, does not report the incident to the police. This may suggest that he receives the assault as a moral ordeal. In view of this consideration Orlick may be described as a kind of *alter ego* who performs a punitive role in relation to Pip.

The attack by the gypsies on Harry remains similarly mysterious since the narrator fails to find a motivation behind it. In its spontaneity the act parallels Orlick's; and Harry, like Pip, expresses puzzlement rather than resentment against the agents of the action. Harry would have reported the incident to Bulsted or to Riversley had he responded to it with the usual spirit of revenge. His silence over the matter is a mystery which perplexes his father. (XLIV, 539)

The moral aspect of the ordeal of the attack on Harry is relatively explicit. It seems as if Meredith, in comparison with Dickens, is unable to maintain detachment towards the inexplicable mystery. When the attack is almost over, Harry says: 'I . . . thought of Germany and my father, and Janet at her window, complacently; raised a child's voice in my throat for mercy, quite inaudible, and accepted my punishment'. (XLVI, 528) Later Harry described the process of interplay between mind and body as a result of the attack: 'The mind's total apathy was the sign of recovering health. Kind nature put that district to sleep while she operated on the disquieted lower functions. I looked on my later self as one observes the massy bearded substances travelling blind along the undercurrent of the stream, clinging to this and that, twirling absurdly'. (XLVI, 530)

The link between the two worlds in which Harry finds himself caught is represented by Kiomi, who undertakes to protect Harry after the attack. The gypsy woman acts as a catalyst between Riversley and Bulsted. She is not like the other gypsy women who belong only to one world. Her response to Harry's situation suggests that she is capable of seeing beyond the limitations of one world or another. She makes Harry's ordeal not only real but also acceptable.

Another character pattern which can be considered Dickensian in origin is that of Edbury whose function in *Harry Richmond* recalls Drummle's in *Great Expectations*. Edbury and Drummle may be viewed as functional equivalents to the gypsies and Orlick in performing a punitive role.

Punishment in Harry's situation is not, however, as complex as it is in Pip's. Janet is restored to Harry after the temporary ordeal brought about through her engagement to Edbury. With Pip the ordeal of his separation from Estella is never undone, and the moral function of the ordeal remains implicit as in the Pip–Orlick relationship.

This pattern of mystery and romance, fused together and integrated into the total experience of the hero, is a characteristic aspect of *Great Expectations* as a *Bildungsroman*. By comparison, melodrama in *Wilhelm Meister* often takes the form of disconnected experience, and remains for the most part a continuation of the eighteenth century picaresque tradition.

In *Harry Richmond* the treatment of melodrama is Dickensian rather than Goethean, and Meredith's main preoccupation was to integrate the melodrama of adventure into the main action of the novel.

Dickens's influence on Meredith goes, however, beyond these particular patterns of theme and character. From Dickens Meredith seems to have obliquely learnt that the frontiers of the *Bildungsroman* are not limited to those of Goethe's *Wilhelm Meister*, or even to those of Dickens's own. Hence comes Meredith's own *Bildungsroman*.

Besides being a different history of father and son, *Harry Richmond* represents a break with Meredith's experimental novels of adventure of the 1860s.[4] It has its origin in the sixties, however, and is first mentioned in a letter to F. M. Evans (5 August 1861) as 'an autobiographical story in view for *Once a Week*'. (1, 95) Another reference to 'an Autobiographic tale' occurs later in a letter to William Hardman (1, 254). In a letter to Augustus Jessopp (18 May 1864), the title of the autobiographic tale is mentioned for the first time: 'I have also in hand an Autobiography. *The Adventures of Richmond Roy, and his friend Contrivance Jack: Being the History of Two Rising Men*:—and to be a spanking bid for popularity on the part of this writer'. (1, 255)[5] In another letter to William Hardman, Meredith writes that: 'Lucas is charmed with the sketch of the autobiography; but owing to certain changes going on in relation to O[nce] a W[eek] he has not yet sent word for me to start away.' (1, 275) It is perhaps due to the 'certain changes' that the sketch neither developed into the planned novel nor found its way into Lucas's journal. Writing again to Augustus Jessopp (7 January 1869), Meredith says: 'I am busy finishing a novel for the *Cornhill Magazine*, one of three or four that are carved out, and waiting'. (1, 412–3) He announces the completion of the novel in another letter to William Hardman (6 July 1870).[6]

The novel did not emerge directly from the original plan for an

autobiographic tale. Examination of the sketch, a MS fragment of
which I was able to examine at the Beinecke Library of Yale
University, shows that the present novel was originally intended 'to
be a spanking bid for popularity'.

The title and the fragmentary sketch suggest that Meredith
intended to use the theme of the career of men rising in the world. In
the summary of the opening chapter, he writes: 'Opening—the
Meeting with Contrivance Jack on Wimbledon Common. His
contrivances: as to letter to be placed by absent friends so that they
are sure to hear from one another—as to ride to London . . .'[7] In
the margin are notes of contrivances to be attributed to Jack:

> How two poor fellows may get money: one by getting the other
> prosecuted for trespass. They toss up.
> How to get money on the road: . . . .
> How to get a lady's picture: by getting it painted and hung up in
> husband's house. The husband sells it, the lover buys.

Chapter v, entitled 'Life in London', and the title of Chapter xv,
'Their Journey to London',[8] further suggest the intention of making
London the main scene of action.

This theme was popular early in the century and continued to be
so in the middle of the century, featuring in fiction from the writing
of Bulwer-Lytton to that of Charles Dickens. In France it was
already well established in the fiction of major writers.

The other aspect of the original plan as revealed by the sketch
which relates to popular practice in fiction, is the sensational nature
of the incidents. From Chapter vi onwards the sketch is overwhelm-
ingly dominated by mystery and adventure. The intrigues of
Chapter vii, for example, are very reminiscent of those of 'Ali Baba
and the Forty Thieves' in *The Arabian Nights*; other incidents of
adventure and murder in the following chapters are reminiscent of
Collins'; and Jack's adventures and contrivances recall those of
Disraeli's Vivian in *Vivian Grey* and Sterling's Arthur in *Arthur
Coningsby*.

The emphasis on sensational incident shows Meredith attempting to follow the popular practice of bringing realism to fiction by
means of descriptive account of incident rather than through
portrayal of character. His experience with *Rhoda Fleming* (1865)
and *Vittoria* (1867), both written about the time when the sketch was
written (presumably in the mid-sixties), seems to have decided

Meredith to stop experimenting with sensational fiction, and in this light the plan, with the sketch, as it exists, ending with Chapter xv, were abandoned.

Meredith declared in a letter to Manville Fenn, editor of *Cassell's Magazine* (12 October 1870), that he had lost interest in the kind of adventures promising to be 'a spanking bid for popularity'. While *Harry Richmond* was running in serial in the *Cornhill Magazine*, Fenn, apparently taken by the adventures of the book, wrote to the publishers inquiring about the author, intending to ask him to write for his own magazine. Meredith received the letter through his publishers and replied:

> I am not absolutely engaged upon any work at present, and am not very anxious to engage myself, but if the proprietors of *Casell's Magazine* should think fit to make a fair offer for a story, and will give me a reasonable time to produce it in, I see no objection to our coming to terms. —I presume that as the Editor of a magazine you want a tale of quick and spirited adventure. I have one in view—the last of the sort I shall write. I am happier when writing in my own vein than in that which seems to please the public. (III, 1703)

The 'tale of quick and spirited adventure', like the sketch sent to Lucas, was doomed to remain unwritten.

The general frame of the story of the sketch survives in *Harry Richmond*; and Richard H. Hudson perhaps overlooks the process of transformation when he remarks that none of the sensational incidents of the sketch appear in *Harry Richmond*. For example, the summary of the fourth chapter of the sketch, 'A Terrible Discovery', describes Richmond Roy going 'to the great house in the great square, of which he believes his father to be the master, taking Contrivance Jack with him, and discovers that his father is but a visiting singing master there; acting a part.' This scene recalls the statue scene in *Harry Richmond*. The summary chapter has marginal notes describing Jack's fears of failure, which recall aspects of the character of Harry's father in the novel. 'Jack on the way describes himself; declares himself of a mighty ambition, but adds that he fears he may turn out a scoundrel, being a ticklish fellow. Has a real fear that he may end badly.'

Incidents, then, survive in the novel, in one way or another, but they acquire a different emphasis. Instead of being a secondary

incident, the history of Richmond Roy and his son becomes a main
concern of the novel. The notion of the son's emancipation from the
father, which is just hinted at in the sketch, is a determining theme
in the novel, where it becomes a matter of developing consciousness
rather than incident.

Adventures feature largely in the novel, but the picaresque aspect
of Harry and even of his father remain the outer aspect of character.
Dr Julius von Karsteg's comment on Harry's mind reveals the
function of adventure in *Harry Richmond*, as distinguished from its
function in sensational fiction: 'You are fortunate if you have a solid
and adventurous mind: most unfortunate if you are a mere
sensational whipster.' (xxix, 316)

The statement of the doctor sums up the main design of *Harry
Richmond*. While the book was running in serial Meredith described
this design to Augustus Jessopp:

> Consider first my scheme as a workman. It is to show you the
> action of minds as well as of fortunes of here and there men and
> women vitally animated by their brains at different periods of
> their lives—and of men and women with something of a look-out
> upon the world and its destinies:—the mortal ones: the divine I
> leave to Doctors of D. Let these far-sighted gentlemen speak on
> such subjects. —I dare say the novel won't be liked, but I know
> my plan, I do my work, and if I am kept very poor I hope to pay
> all in time. (1, 451)

The letter evidently shows that Meredith intended the adventures
of the book (acts of fortune) to serve as incidents of intrinsic interest.
The hero's analysis of the nature and significance of the acts of
fortune is what results in his understanding of himself, out of which
the acts of mind are shaped. This interplay of the two kinds of acts
recalls Henry James's well-known description of character and
incident as demonstration and embodiment of one another. It
similarly stands as a main preoccupation in *Wilhelm Meister*.
Wilhelm talks about 'inner circumstances' and 'outer circumstances' in *Hamlet*. Book III of *Wilhelm Meister* concludes with an
outcry concerning chance or destiny. The First Stranger refers to
chance as 'the element which we use'; and the Second Stranger
refers to destiny as 'the element in which we live'.

The two aspects of action in the novel can be identified with the terms romance and realism, which, from the technical point of view, may be described as the proportional distance between the narrator and the object of narration. In their use in the novel, Meredith achieves considerable clarity, unlike his confusion of tragedy and comedy in *Richard Feverel*. The design of the book may be viewed as an attempt to accommodate the English romance to the German *Bildungsroman*.

Richard Feverel feels himself to be the centre of the world: Harry Richmond explores the world in order to find himself. His character grows as he comes to understand and acknowledge his relationship to the forces which threaten to control his life, and frees himself from their domination. These forces are represented in the father and grandfather between whom Harry finds himself a subject of dispute. Squire Beltham is traditional, secure and well placed in society. He wants Harry to inherit Riversley and marry Janet in order to increase and consolidate his wealth. He tries to prepare Harry for the world of reality. Roy, on the other hand, is a rising man who dreams of wealth and power. He introduces his son to fashionable London and to Germany, and transports Harry to a world of fantasy.

Harry's early life is dominated by his father. During the periods that Harry lives at Riversley, he remains uncompliant to his grandfather's plans, and longs to be with his father.

Roy provides for Harry an enchanting environment of romance, and of fantasy. To amuse the infant Harry, he arranges a daily Punch and Judy show.[9] He makes story-books come alive for the child through his gift for acting, producing and appreciating comedy: 'Then we read the Arabian Nights together, or, rather, he read them to me, often acting out the incidents as we rode or drove abroad.' (IV, 38) And again:

> To divert me during my recovery from measles, he one day hired an actor in a theatre, and put a cloth round his neck, and seated him in a chair, rubbed his chin with soap, and played the part of the Barber over him, and I have never laughed so much in my life. Poor Mrs. Waddy got her hands at her sides, and kept on gasping, 'Oh, sir! oh!' while the Barber hurried away from the half-shaved young man to consult his pretended astrolabe in the next room, where we heard him shouting the sun's altitude, and consulting its willingness for the impatient young man to be

further shaved; and back he came, seeming refreshed to have
learnt the sun's favourable opinion, and gabbling at an immense
rate, full of barber's business. The servants were allowed to be
spectators; but as soon as the young man was shaved, my father
dismissed them with the tone of a master. No wonder they loved
him. (IV, 39)

As Wilhelm saw life acted out as a theatrical drama, Harry saw
romance illustrated. So did David Copperfield, who was similarly
enchanted by *The Arabian Nights*.[10]

But Meredith exploits the theme of romance by integrating the
world of boyhood fable into the preoccupying theme of father and
son. This is what generates the twofold effect of Roy's upbringing:
that Harry is made a recipient of excitement rather than a
participant in action, and that he is made dependent on his father
for interest in life. The narrator's comment on the Punch and Judy
shows illustrates the latter: '. . . yet here again his genius defeated
his kind intentions; for happening once to stand by my side during
the progress of the show, he made it so vivid to me by what he said
and did, that I saw no fun in it without him: I used to dread the
heralding crow of Punch if he was away, and cared no longer for
wooden heads being knocked ever so hard.' (II, 16) In his growth,
therefore, Harry has to find means of breaking this bond. At the
same time, the high level of stimulation and excitement offered by
his father can be seen as contributing to Harry's appetite for
adventure in later life.

In the life of Kiomi and her people Harry finds romance and
mystery. His frequent visits to the gypsies signify his quest for
freedom, and his casual interest in fortune-telling overlies a serious
concern with the future. Harry's curiosity drives him to question
whether the acts of mind can reveal acts of fortune in advance of
their happening.

Another source of mystery and romance is Captain Welsh, who
rescues Harry and Temple from supposed moral danger in London
and offers them a spiritual apprenticeship. His utterance, 'I pray for
no storm, but, by the Lord's mercy, for a way to your hearts through
fire or water' (XIII, 164), may be considered a symbolic allusion to
the separate courses of the boys' adventures.[11] (Both the gypsies and
Captain Welsh play a part in the resolution of the plot later on.)

The mysterious nature of the acts of fortune by which Harry is
confronted is not only appealing in itself, but the coincidence by

which they eventually unite him with his father instils in Harry a
sense of being guided by Providence: 'Recent events had given me
the assurance that in my search for my father I was subject to a
special governing direction. I had aimed at the Bench—missed it—
been shipped across sea and precipitated into the arms of friends
who had seen him and could tell me I was on his actual track, only
blindly, and no longer blindly now.' (xv, 178)

The romantic nature of Harry's search for his father is conveyed
earlier in the book, when he compares him to Ulysses, and himself to
Telemachus: 'Telemachus is the one I mean. He was in search of his
father. He found him at last. Upon my honour, Temple, when I
think of it, I'm ashamed to have waited so long. I call that luxury
I've lived in senseless. Yes! while I was uncertain whether my father
had enough to eat or not.' (xi, 140) At this stage, Harry is too much
involved in the romantic adventure to need Colonel Goodwin's
advice: 'Under your grandfather's care you have a career before
you, a fine fortune in prospect, everything a young man can wish
for. And I must tell you candidly, you run great risk of missing all
these things by hunting your father to earth. Give yourself a little
time: reflect on it.' (xiv, 171)

Father and son are reunited in the statue scene, which marks the
culmination of the comedy in which Harry depends on his father. A
phase in their relationship where Harry becomes more detached
now begins.

Roy's schemes are revealed as contrivances rather than magic as
his son grows older. He asks Harry to be careful not to offend the
squire: 'Good acres—good anchorage; good coffers—good har-
bourage.' Like the squire, he believes that 'on money you mount',
but while the squire can offer Harry wealth, Roy can offer nothing
more than his fantasy of how to acquire it. He justifies his
extravagance in entertaining half-pay English military officers on
the grounds that he hoped it would teach Harry the importance of
having money, and that it could be regarded as a contribution to the
defence of England against the French, as one of the officers, Major
Dykes, was on a mission to search for a new and terrible weapon
believed to be in French possession.[12]

Roy confides to his son that 'the entire course of his life was a
grand plot, resembling an unfinished piece of architecture, which
might, at a future day, prove the wonder of the world'. Even when
he acknowledges his precarious financial position, his optimism
dominates: 'My darling boy! my curse through life has been that the

sense of weight in money is a sense I am and was born utterly a stranger to. The consequence is, my grandest edifices fall; there is no foundation for them. Not that I am worse, understand me, than under a temporary cloud, and the blessing of heaven has endowed me with a magnificent constitution.' (XIX, 222)

The effect of Harry's trip to the continent is that he gains a sharper eye for understanding the world and his father. With his father once again in the debtors' prison, he reflects: 'His exuberant cheerfulness and charming playfulness were always fascinating. His visions of our glorious future enchained me. How it was that something precious had gone out of my life, I could not comprehend.' (XX, 229)

Subsequently, as contrivance follows contrivance, Harry's attitude to his father is clarified. Following the failure of Roy's projected marriage with Anna Penrhys, Harry's state of mind is described again: 'The vitality of the delusion I cherished was therefore partly extinct; not so the love; yet the love of him could no longer shake itself free from oppressive shadows.' (XXII, 258)[13]

One consequence of Harry's adult view of his father is that he becomes free to be active rather than passive in his experience. The two states make different demands on the narrator, the one an account of incidents, the other, analysis of situations. As Harry comes to view his life more closely, the range of the acts of fortune is narrowed down, while that of the acts of mind expands. This makes action in the latter part of the book slow, bringing about Meredith's remarks to William Hardman, when the serialisation of the book was coming to completion (2 November 1871):

> It struck me that a perusal without enforced pauses might lead you to see that the conception was full and good, and was honestly worked out. I resisted every temptation to produce great and startling effects (after the scene of the Statue, which was permissible in art, as coming from a boy and coloured by a boy's wonder). Note as you read, the gradual changes of the growing Harry, in his manner of regarding his father and the world. I have carried it so far as to make him perhaps dull towards adolescence and young manhood, except to one *studying* the narrative—as in the scenes with Dr. Julius. Such effects are deadly when appearing in a serial issue. (I, 453–4)

The adventures of the latter part of the book centre mainly around Harry's involvements with Ottilia and Janet, and it is through his developing relationship with these two that he acquires the self-understanding characteristic of the *Bildungsroman* hero.

Ottilia provides a clear contrast to Janet, just as the imaginative Roy is contrasted with the matter-of-fact squire. She stands for longing in Harry in the same way Janet stands for achievement. Harry thought Janet commonplace: that she 'talked of love in a ludicrous second-hand way'. (xx, 227) Discussing with Heriot the ideal image of woman, he says: 'I wanted bloom and mystery, a woman shifting like the light with evening and night and dawn, and sudden fire. Janet was bald to the heart inhabiting me then, as if quite shaven. She could speak her affectionate mind as plain as print, and it was dull print facing me, not the arches of the sunset' (xxiii, 260). Janet's straightforward character is reflected in her spontaneous expression of her feelings. On Harry's birthday her greeting is: 'A thousand happy years to you, and me to see them, if you don't mind. I'm first to wish it, I'm certain!' (xxiii, 263) In contrast, Ottilia is subtle.[14] Her expressions are provocative and exciting to Harry. He struggles to grasp the meaning, for example, of her 'violets are over':

> I sat and thrilled from head to foot with a deeper emotion than joy. Not I, but a detached self allied to the careering universe and having life in it.
>
> 'Violets are over.'
>
> The first strenuous effort of my mind was to grasp the meaning, subtle as odour, in these words. Innumerable meanings wreathed away unattainable to thought. (xxvii, 293)

As in the early days of his life, Harry becomes the shuttlecock of his emotions. This invites the criticism of slow-moving action and 'the near-circular nature of Harry's growth'.[15] Whereas, however, Harry's earlier oscillation is determined by time, in that this was necessary for him to develop sufficiently to be able to define his relationship with his father, his later oscillation results from the division in his mind. Two sides of Harry's character become associated with Ottilia and Janet respectively:

> I thought of Janet—she made me gasp for air; of Ottilia, and she made me long for earth. Sharp, as I write it, the distinction smote

me. I might have been divided by an electrical shot into two
halves, with such an equal force was I drawn this way and that,
pointing nowhither. To strangle the thought of either one of them
was like the pang of death; yet it did not strike me that I loved the
two: they were apart in my mind, actually as if I had been
divided. (L, 575–6)[16]

Complex imagery aptly reflects the indecisive nature of his
thinking:

I awoke with a sailor's song on my lips. Looking out of window at
the well-known features of the heaths and dark firs, and waning
oak copses, and the shadowy line of the downs stretching their
long whale backs South to West, it struck me that I had been
barely alive of late. Indeed one who consents to live as I had done,
in a hope and a retrospect, will find his life slipping between the
two, like the ships under the striding Colossus. (XXXVI, 394)

Harry is temporarily but symbolically reconciled when Janet and
Ottilia meet. Ironically, they ignore him when they are together. It
was evident to him that they 'conversed much and perhaps
intimately'. Their meeting symbolises the healing of the rift in
Harry's mind, and foreshadows his reconciliation.

Harry's attraction to Ottilia leads him to explore the power of
reason. Ottilia and her mentor, Dr Julius von Karsteg, teach him to
argue. The most significant result of Harry's involvement with
Ottilia lies in his learning about his limitations.[17] He is incapable of
marriage with Ottilia. Her rank and state, and Harry's oscillation
have been assumed by critics to be the reasons for this. It is not clear
in the novel before Ottilia's revelation in the final chapter (which
will be discussed later) what the real significance of their failure to
marry is. In the realisation by the mature Harry that he cannot
fulfil this aspiration, *Harry Richmond* draws close to *Wilhelm
Meister*; Goethe wrote to Schiller that the book 'sprang from a dim
feeling of the great truth that man often seeks that which nature has
rendered impossible to him'.[18]

Harry's training in the use of reason is considered to enable him to
bear his disappointment in love. Unlike Richard and Werther,
whose disappointment in love ends in death, Harry is able to use this
experience for further learning about himself. (This may be
considered similar to the theme of the hero in failure, who is given

full presentation, though in a different context, in *Beauchamp's Career*.)

While Harry is unable, by efforts of his own will, to resolve the conflict within himself, acts of fortune intervene. The conflict is resolved by the coalescence of the acts of mind with the acts of fortune by means of entanglement and disentanglement of plot. The squire, who lives all his life insisting on a match between Harry and Janet, dies. Janet is engaged to marry Edbury. Consequently Harry undergoes a trial, the detailed description of which is suppressed from the revised edition of the book, which first appeared in 1886.[19] He reflects on the nature of his oscillation between Ottilia and Janet and comes to see himself more clearly in relation to them: 'Ottilia's worldly and intellectual rank both had been constantly present to temper my cravings; but Janet was on my level—mentally a trifle below it, morally above—hard as metal if she liked.' (p. 247)[20] With Janet's engagement to Edbury, a new consciousness emerges in Harry: 'I won her; she was tasteless. I lost her: she was all human life.' (p. 248)

Thus, when Harry's thinking leads him to a reconciliation with Janet, he becomes unable to act on his feelings because Edbury's proposal—an act of fortune—intervenes.

Two acts of fortune which occur earlier in the book, are now recalled to lead to the resolution of plot. Kiomi helps Edbury to learn the whereabouts of Mabel and the ship; Captain Welsh, as he had done earlier with Harry and Temple, makes Edbury 'take the voyage for discipline's sake and "his soul's health"'.

The two incidents are symbolic in fusing romance and realism. Earlier the romance of the trip provides the ecstasy of action, whereas here it suggests tension. The difference is articulated by the romance of boyhood and the disillusionment of maturity, which is the most characteristic feature of the development of the *Bildungsroman* hero. Captain Welsh's belief that he is rescuing Harry and Temple from corruption in the early part of the book may seem lacking in probability, but the similar act in connection with Edbury is not so. Thus, romance progresses from fantasy to reality, enacting Harry's own progression in life. At the same time, the process of change is animated by the sea imagery. As before, when Harry 'dreamed he was in a ship of cinnamon-wood upon a sea that rolled mighty, but smooth immense broad waves, and tore thing from thing without a sound or a hurt' (1, 14), the sea in Harry's maturity symbolises the dissolution of life. Ottilia says to Harry that their 'souls were caught together on the sea'. (XXXI, 331) Reflecting on his love for Ottilia, Harry says: 'I looked back on the thought like the ship on its furrow through the waters, and saw every mortal perplexity, and death under. My love of Ottilia delusion? Then life was delusion!'. (XXXVIII, 434) At last, the sea puts an end to Edbury's life.

Kiomi's intervention is also brought into reality, as the mysterious possibility of fortune-telling is tested in her guidance of Edbury to Mabel and the ship.

The resolution of conflict involves the bringing together of the acts of mind and the acts of fortune. Meredith is here tackling the issue which figures largely in his later fiction, of the conflict between the ideal (awareness and desire) and the real (the will to put the ideal into action). Harry is able to modify his evaluation of the acts of fortune, which earlier he had blamed for what displeased him. In his maturity, Harry's reflection suggests that he now sees circumstances as reduced in function to making the ideal (what is grasped by the acts of the mind) real: 'I was still subject to the relapses of a not perfectly right nature, as I perceived when glancing back at my thought of "An odd series of accidents!" which was but a disguised fashion of attributing to Providence the particular concern in my fortunes: an impiety and a folly! This is the temptation of those who are rescued and made happy by circumstances.' (LVI, 680–1)[21]

The contribution of the acts of mind to the reconciliation are illuminated by Ottilia when Harry asks what takes her most in Janet.

> Her courage. And it is of a kind that may knot up every other virtue worth having. I have impulses, and am capable of desperation, but I have no true courage: so I envy and admire, even if I have to blame her; for I know that this possession of hers, which identifies her and marks her from the rest of us, would bear the ordeal of fire. I can imagine the qualities I have most pride in withering and decaying under a prolonged trial. I cannot conceive her courage failing. Perhaps because I have it not myself I think it the rarest of precious gifts. It seems to me to imply one half, and to dispense with the other. (LVI, 683)

Ottilia's confession brings about the climactic revelation of the book. It defines the power which has been suspending action. She uses the term courage to express what Harry vaguely conceived as the will to act. Ottilia, the daughter of reason, studies Janet, the daughter of nature, and becomes disillusioned about the limitations of reason. Despite its powerful insight, Ottilia implies, reason cannot generate courageous action.

This revelation implies that Harry's relationship with Ottilia was illusory: that marriage was never a possibility. The illusory relationship is not morally condemned; indeed Meredith is at pains to avoid moral scrutiny of Harry's response to Ottilia's love. He omits passages in the *MS* which reveal dishonesty and pride, for example, a passage which shows Harry to be responsible for turning away from Ottilia: 'I turned sharp round and performed a circuit of the old pine promontory of the temple of the statue, Bella Vista; and so avoided her, pretending to think she meditated and should not be disturbed'. (*MS*, II, 694)

Passages are also suppressed which show Harry reflecting on his behaviour and blaming himself in the belief that his rejection of Ottilia was prompted by folly, while Ottilia's attitude was the outcome of generous feelings: 'In vain I write round and round my confession of folly; the admonition of it will not be diluted. There stood the woman, the purest lady of earth, my prize, the bravest and truest Princess ever born, she who had just acknowledged me to be her lover! and I rode off!' (*MS*, II, 697)

The withholding of Ottilia's revelation to such a late stage in the book enables Meredith to portray education through experience. Neither Harry nor Ottilia is to blame for their past suffering, for it arose out of the testing of their rational education through experience, and thus consists of a stage in the process of growth to self-understanding.

Harry's disillusionment with reason is seen in his reconsideration of Janet, whom he used to think plain of character because of her plain vocabulary: 'Happily for us both, my wits had been sharpened enough to know that there is more in men and women than the stuff they utter'. (LVI, 682) (Meredith alludes here to the problem of language falling short of character revelation, which is fully presented in Chapter 5.

That the experiences of Ottilia and Harry transcend the limitations of reason is a conclusion which invalidates Norman Kelvin's thesis that the Princess, 'in becoming an ideal for Janet, plays the same role in her life as she plays in Harry's. In both, she is the moral touchstone, and Harry and Janet are actually converted to her image, giving up, in the process, their old irrational passions and wishes.'[22]

Kelvin seems to have over-emphasised the impact of the Professor's instruction on Harry and Ottilia, without realising either that it has not led them to the same position, or that Ottilia herself shares the disillusionment with reason. It is true that Ottilia subjects her emotions to rational analysis, and that even when she confesses her love to Harry she ascribes it to the weakness which 'has come upon her'. (xxx, 326) That there is no suggestion in the book that she is satisfied in her marriage to the German Prince with whom she shares an interest in scholarship, indirectly suggests that she knows from her own experience with her husband, as well as with Harry and Janet, the limited rôle of reason in marriage.

Harry's vacillation is not brought to an end by a rational decision on his part. At the same time, 'Janet either did or affected to weigh the princess's reasonings; and she did not evade the task of furnishing a full reply. Her resolution was unchanged.' (LV, 665) The union between Harry and Janet is not, then, the triumph of the rational over the irrational. Nor is it the rejection of the rational mind. There is rather a sense of reconciliation with the illusion that has been lost. He continues to feel its value, while, at the same time, he accepts the present situation. Ottilia and Harry acknowledge the loss of ideal love with dignified resignation and without recrimination. It is felt that they finally part as friends. Between their early innocent adoption of the rational and their realisation of its limitation lies experience. It is important, however, to realise that the fruit of experience is not prudence. This is what, in general, distinguishes *Harry Richmond* from *Richard Feverel*; *Great Expectations* from *David Copperfield*; and *Wilhelm Meister* from *Werther*. The absence of prudence as a conclusion in *Great Expectations* and *Harry Richmond* is one major characteristic which distinguishes Dickens's and Meredith's practices in the *Bildungsroman* from those of other writers of the time such as Bulwer-Lytton and Disraeli.

The autobiographical novel raises a particular problem in connection with the resolution of the plot. As the narrator comes closer to the point where he started the narrative it becomes less easy for him to dissociate himself from the flow of experience, and consequently it becomes more difficult to avoid immediate judgement and self-justification. Any specific ending, then, will normally tempt the reader to reconsider the earlier life of the narrator within the limits of a particular ending. This can lead to the subjection of the whole life of the narrator to moral judgement and to the under-estimation of growth and experience in the narrative.

In *Great Expectations*, for example, Dickens was faced with just this problem of ending. The book was originally concluded by the interview between Pip and Estella where Pip was assured by the disillusion in Estella about Miss Havisham's teaching. Later Dickens changed this conclusion, as is well-known, at the recommendation of Bulwer-Lytton, who objected to 'a close that should leave Pip a solitary man'. The ending (as it now stands) concludes with the union between Estella and Pip which is as much suggestive of sorrow or of joy as the reader wishes to see.[23]

Meredith's preoccupation with the question of how to end can be traced as early as the three chapters (XIV, XV and XVI of the first edition) which are suppressed from the revised edition (1886). At that point in the narrative Meredith perhaps contemplated the idea of bringing the conclusion to an unhappy ending. This would have required the marrying of Janet to Edbury and the leaving of Harry without either Janet or Ottilia. But Meredith's lack of confidence in his ability to tie up subplots with the main stories may have prevented him from going further with the incident, for he is not, for example, as skilful in this way as Dickens. He cannot develop the episode of Edbury and Janet and then integrate it into the main story as Dickens integrated the subplot of Drummle and Estella into the main story of *Great Expectations*.

However the abandonment of a possible elaborate subplot is not inconsistent with Meredith's rejection of the sketch of the book discussed earlier in this chapter where he perhaps felt his incapacity to integrate sensational incidents and character. At the same time Meredith's past experience with *Rhoda Fleming* (where the introduction of incidents and subplots towards the end results in melodrama) may have taught him not to repeat the practice.

Meredith's anxiety that the novel should not be brought to an unhappy ending led him to leave unelaborated some incidents which might have prejudiced the realisation of this aim. To this end, Meredith also sacrificed three chapters in which the change in Harry's attitude to Janet is explicit and involves more stringent self-criticism on his part. The effect of these suppressions is to leave undetermined the attitude of the narrator towards the latter stages of his development. (This parallels the suppression of self-criticism in connection with Ottilia, as demonstrated earlier from the revisions on the *MSS*.)

Another result of the revision is more technical: by the suppression of three chapters dominated mainly by dialogue the proportion of narrative to dialogue is greatly increased. Meredith perhaps realised that telling, rather than dramatising, is best for concluding scenes because it provides the narrator with more control over the movement of action as well as making the later life of the narrator less vulnerable to moral judgement.

In its general pattern the ending of *Harry Richmond* has much in common with that of *Great Expectations*. The scene in which Harry and Janet are brought together leaving Riversley on fire recalls that of Pip and Estella walking hand in hand 'out of the ruined place'. The disappearance of Richmond Roy in *Harry Richmond* recalls that of Miss Havisham in *Great Expectations*. Another common pattern can be traced in the background motif of mist and fire. In *Great Expectations* the action of the novel falls between the rising of the morning mists and the rising of the evening mists. In *Harry Richmond* action begins with Roy's persistent knocking at the door and Squire Beltham waking up, 'swearing by his Lord Harry he had just dreamed of fire, and muttering of buckets', and ends with the fire burning down Riversley and with Richmond Roy caught in the fire.[24]

In tone, however, the ending of *Harry Richmond* contrasts with that of *Great Expectations*. There is as much celebration in one as there is suffering in the other. In either novel the ending has a counter-undertone besides the dominant one.

However the element of suffering in the ending of *Harry Richmond* might be criticised. One wonders how much justification there is for having Riversley left on fire and Harry's father caught in the middle of it. For Harry and Janet Riversley is not, for example, like Satis House for Pip and Estella—a symbol of destruction. Nor is Richmond Roy like Miss Havisham.

The burning of Riversley may be justified if it is taken as a place which will always be reminiscent of an early painful experience where Harry was a shuttlecock between father and grandfather. Or the justification may be on the grounds that Riversley is an object of disputable property between father and grandfather: each, in his own way, wishes Harry to be its inheritor. In that case its burning may be interpreted to suggest Harry's complete emancipation from the last bond of father and son. But the objection to this interpretation lies in the fact that Harry has already outgrown the obligation of dependence on his father.

However the scene of fire remains in itself suggestive of the dignified silence which broods over the conclusion. Harry and Janet stand before the scene awe-stricken but uncommitted.

> The Grange was burning in two great wings, that soared in flame-tips and columns of crimson smoke, leaving the central hall and chambers untouched as yet, but alive inside with mysterious ranges of lights, now curtained, now made bare—a feeble contrast to the savage blaze to right and left, save for the wonder aroused as to its significance. These were soon cloaked. Dead sable reigned in them, and at once a jet of flame gave the whole vast building to destruction. My wife thrust her hand in mine. Fire at the heart, fire at the wings—our old home stood in that majesty of horror which freezes the limbs of men, bidding them look and no more.
>
> 'What has Riversley done to deserve this?' I heard Janet murmur to herself. 'His room!' she said, when at the South-east wing, where my old grandfather had slept, there burst a glut of flame. We drove down to the park and along the carriage-road to the first red line of gazers. (LVI, 684)

Richmond Roy meets his end as he runs to rescue Aunt Dorothy whom he assumes to be at Riversley. He is tragically reconciled to death—but with his good intentions and his fantasy still un-separated. His act may be accounted for within the general picture of 'the action of minds as well as of fortunes'. But the tone remains pathetic if not tragic. Harry and Janet gather that a great reception had been prepared for them by his father: 'But the house must have been like a mine, what with the powder, the torches, the devices in paper and muslin, and the extraordinary decorations fitted up to celebrate our return in harmony with my father's fancy.' (LVI, 684)[25] The scene is suggestive. It implies Roy's rejoicing in the happy union between Harry and Janet and, at the same time, his satisfaction with the fulfilment of his scheme of inheriting Riversley. Harry's comment on the celebration as fancy further suggests the sharp division in attitude to reality between father and son.

In *Harry Richmond* the relationship between father and son is defined successfully and without the confusion met in *Richard Feverel*. Harry develops; his father does not. This is perhaps how Meredith wished to present the history of father and son earlier in *Richard Feverel*. The fact that Meredith wrote another history of father and son after more than ten years suggests that the theme was still dear to him. By this time Meredith had worked through his personal ordeal—and, perhaps more important, he had found the appropriate form: the *Bildungsroman*. It is striking that Dickens also had written a second autobiographical novel a decade or so after his first—and that he too had already found the same form most appropriate to his artistic needs.

4 *Beauchamp's Career*: Wider Horizon

Meredith saw *Beauchamp's Career* as an attempt to break away from the novel 'of the real story telling order' of the 1860s, and he referred to it as a 'monstrous innovation' which, as he says in his letter to Conway, has 'no powerful stream of adventure' (1, 485).

His earliest reference to *Beauchamp's Career* occurs in a letter to his friend Maxse, presumably written earlier than Christmas 1870. 'I have just finished the History of the inextinguishable Sir Harry Firebrand of the Beacon—Knight Errant of the 19th century, into which mirror you may look and see—My dear Fred and his loving friend, George Meredith.' (1, 352)

The letter has aroused speculation among critics as to Meredith's reason for abandoning an early incomplete novel, and as to the identification of the autobiographical element in the printed novel. Edward Clodd, for example, claims that the letter refers to a lost incomplete version of the novel which Meredith abandoned because of criticisms of its increasing obscurity.[1] That Meredith did not fulfil the plans described in the letter is an indication of his intention at that time to give up the more sensational type of fiction he had attempted in the 1860s.

Viscountess Milner writes that in her talk with Meredith in 1904 she was told of a plan for a book which he had had for a long time. He mentioned to her that he had worked it out in some detail and given it to H. G. Wells, regretting that he had been unable to write it himself.

The plan as outlined is in the vein of Meredith's fiction of the 1860s. It is not unlikely that its idea is a version of the 'Knight-errant of the 19th century', reshaped by this time in the fashion of science fiction:

> It is the story of the Don Quixote of the future. A man
> immensely rich, imbued with Herbert Spencer's ideas, full of the

all-importance of the future and its problems, always dwelling on them, always working at them. Nothing is too great and nothing is too small for his zeal. He has a scheme, worked out in conjunction with men of science and enthusiasts, for moving the Earth. He thinks that as the Sun gets colder the planets will be drawn closer and closer, and that the Earth will run the risk of being burnt, so he has a plan for moving the whole Earth out of its orbit into some other fixed star's neighbourhood![2]

There are elements of the knightly theme in *Beauchamp's Career*. In the atmosphere of alarm concerning a French invasion, the young Beauchamp, dutifully but unrealistically defies the French challenge: he is 'the champion of his country'. The Crimean War features in the novel as the incident which reveals Beauchamp's chivalry. He is one of the warriors whose bravery made up for the humiliation of the defeat of the army. Another aspect of chivalrous behaviour is seen in Beauchamp's willingness to take dramatic risks on behalf of individuals as well as for his country: he saves Roland's life, undertakes the risky adventure of trying to save Renée from an unfortunate marriage; he is honoured for life-saving in Bevisham waters and finally dies while saving an urchin from drowning.

Such acts of bravery are related briefly in the novel. Sensational incident is reduced to a minimum, serving as a background to the main action which is the inner life of the character. In abandoning the plan for a novel of knight-errantry and adopting that of Beauchamp's career, Meredith turns from the presentation of types to specificity in theme and character. Knight-errantry is replaced by the treatment of 'men, and the ideas of men, which are . . . actually the motives of men in a greater degree than their appetites'. (I, 7) The tone of the novel is serious. In his letter to Conway, Meredith describes the novel—which is 'philosophical–political'—as 'an attempt to show the forces round a young man of the present day, in England, who would move them, and finds them unalterably solid, though it is seen in the end that he does not altogether fail, has not lived quite in vain.' He considers 'his History a picture of the time—taking its mental action, and material ease, and indifference, to be a necessary element of the picture.' (I, 485)

Meredith sets out his strategy for the presentation of this picture of the time in the prefatory paragraph of Chapter IV (38–40), where he emphasises Beauchamp's struggle against his England, 'the greater power of the two', who denies her son 'a conceivable epic'.

The paragraph warns readers against mistaking the author's purpose. It implies Meredith's preoccupation with plotless action, or what he describes as 'artless art and monstrous innovation to present so wilful a figure'.

Emphasis on Beauchamp's individuality leads Meredith to define the distance between character and the omniscient narrator in such a way as to satisfy the demand of realism. He asserts his detachment from the hero with the pretence that Beauchamp's character itself rejects the authorial personage:

> 'For me, I have so little command over him, that in spite of my nursery tastes, he drags me whither he lists. It is artless art and monstrous innovation to present so wilful a figure, but were I to create a striking fable for him, and set him off with scenic effects and contrasts, it would be only a momentary tonic to you, to him instant death. He could not live in such an atmosphere.' (IV, 39)

Earlier in the book he discards what Barbara Hardy calls the dogmatic form or the categories imposed by the author on his characters:[3] 'I give you the position of the country undisturbed by any moralising of mine,' Meredith says. 'I must try to paint for you what is, not what I imagine.' (I, 6) He is here certainly sharing the tendency of contemporary writers to avoid direct intervention of the author's voice in his writing.[4]

Meredith uses 'Beauchampism' as a key term of his own to describe his character presentation. He declares that Beauchampism stands 'for nearly everything which is the obverse of Byronism'; that is, he intends to handle the theme of heroism in accordance with the demands of realism. Beauchamp is distinguished from the Byronic hero principally in that his rebellion against society is motivated by concern for social change and a sense of duty, and not by self-assertion. In his article 'Byron and the Modern World', Bertrand Russell criticised the social consequences of the romantic passion of the Byronic hero in that 'the type of man encouraged by romanticism, especially of the Byronic variety, is violent and anti-social, an anarchic rebel or a conquering tyrant'.[5] Russell remarks that when 'the aristocratic philosophy of rebellion' in Byronic heroism stands against the world, it 'takes the form of Titanic cosmic self-assertion, or, in those who retain some superstition of Satanism'.[6] Meredith demonstrates Beauchamp's differences from the Byronic hero by his rejection of opportunities to indulge in romance, either in his relationship with Renée or in following a career on the sea. Furthermore, the difference is emphasised in Meredith's comment that Beauchamp 'despises the pomades and curling-irons of modern romance' despite 'every inducement to offer himself for a romantic figure. (IV, 39)

In its opposition to Byronism, Beauchampism is allied to Carlylean heroism. Beauchamp's 'favourite author', we know, 'was one writing of Heroes'. (II, 22) Beauchamp had a 'veneration of heroes, living and dead', and a 'reverence for men of deeds'. (I, 12–13) Among others he admires a George-Foxite, who, he tells his uncle, 'speaks wisely . . . like a prophet: and he speaks on behalf of the poor as much as of the country'. (4, 38)[7] Beauchamp's concept of heroism takes a decisive turn when he meets Dr Shrapnel. He says to Cecilia:

> 'I have had my heroes before. You know how I loved Robert Hall: his death is a gap in my life. He is a light for fighting Englishmen—who fight with the sword. But the scale of the war, the cause, and the end in view, raise Dr Shrapnel above the bravest I have ever had the luck to meet. Soldiers and sailors have their excitement to keep them up to the mark; praise and rewards. He is in his eight-and-sixtieth year, and he has never received anything but obloquy for his pains. Half of the small fortune he has goes in charities and subscriptions. Will that touch you? But I think little of that, and so does he. Charity is a common duty. The dedication of a man's life and whole mind to a cause, there's heroism.' (XXXII, 358)

In his hero-worship, Beauchamp is Carlylean. Carlyle believed that the act of hero-worship is in itself heroic. He describes its beneficial effects:

> Veneration of great men is perennial in the nature of man; this in all times, especially in these, is one of the blessedest facts predicable of him. In all times, even in these seemingly so disobedient times, 'it remains a blessed fact, so cunningly has Nature ordered it, *that whatsoever man ought to obey, he cannot but obey.* Show the dullest clodpole, show the haughtiest featherhead, that a soul higher than himself is actually here; were his knees stiffened into brass, he must down and worship.'[8]

The Carlylean view of hero-worship as a purging of the egoism of

Byronism is seen in Beauchamp's study of heroes in order to control his conceit. (I, 12)

Carlyle, like Meredith, objects to the Byronic rejection of society. It is for this reason that his discussion of heroism centres on the past, on accomplished action. Carlyle's views on heroism can only be applied dogmatically to a present situation: they become a doctrine, or a new religion in which, as Eugene Goodheart remarks, 'the new godhead is society, and the new form of worship is doing the work of the world'.[9]

In Beauchamp's career, however, Meredith transcends the dogma of Carlyle. Beauchamp's heroism is not presented as leading to a predetermined harmonious reconciliation. His ideals go on existing although they are in conflict with the reality of society. Failure and the subsequent emerging consciousness form an essential characteristic of Beauchamp's heroism. Unlike the Carlylean hero, he has no monopoly of divine and absolute truth to lead him into the right course of action, but has to test out the practicality of his ideals in order to evaluate them. In his letter, (I, 485) Meredith draws attention to Beauchamp's 'certain drama of self-conquest', and to the imperfections, which, by comparison with the Carlylean, individualise his heroism. Beauchamp has a private life as well as devotion to public duty. His character is revealed through the interplay of the two, which presents his drama of self-conquest, rather than through a confident and inspired pre-destined heroism.

Beauchamp maintains his private passions even where they are not in accord with public duty. He holds the ideal, which he explains to Renée, that there should be room for both freedom of the heart and duty to the country. His response to her message from France during the election demonstrates his intention to live out this ideal. The consequences of this, as well as many other missed opportunities for action, lead him to realise, as he confesses to Cecilia, that he 'can't do two things at a time—make love and carry on my taskwork'. (XLVII, 539) It is important to note that this realisation does not bring disillusion or lead Beauchamp to discard his ideal.

Aspects of *Beauchamp's Career* as a study of the interplay of private and public life can be considered with reference to its close contemporary, *Felix Holt*, in which George Eliot states that she intends to deal with this theme: 'These social changes in Treby parish are comparatively public matters, and this history is chiefly

concerned with the private lot of a few men and women; but there is
no private life which has not been determined by a wider public
life'. (III, 72)[10]

While the picture of Beauchamp's political involvement is seen to
develop progressively from his youthful patriotic aspirations, in
conjunction with current events and through the private relationships he makes, Felix's political motivation appears inconsistent
with the rest of his life. This is seen in trying to combine the career of
the entrepreneur with the notion of 'going shares with the
unlucky'. (XXVII, 36) It is often not clear whether Felix is a rebel, an
ascetic or an egoist: 'And the finest fellow of all would be the one
who could be glad to have lived because the world was chiefly
miserable, and his life had come to help some one who needed it. He
would be the man who had the most powers and the fewest selfish
wants. But I'm not up to the level of what I see to be best. I'm often a
hungry discontented fellow.' (XXVII, 35) He expresses a desire for
escapism: 'Oh, I shall go away as soon as I can to some large
town . . . some ugly, wicked, miserable place. I want to be a
demagogue of a new sort; an honest one, if possible, who will tell the
people they are blind and foolish, and neither flatter them nor fatten
on them.' (XXVII, 41) Finally, his radicalism seems to be overcome
by the established condition of the time, and he speaks more in terms
of the philosophy of economic liberalism than of radicalism:

> 'I have my heritage—an order I belong to. I have the blood of a
> line of handicraftsmen in my veins, and I want to stand up for the
> lot of the handicraftsmen as a good lot, in which a man may be
> better trained to all the best functions of his nature than if he
> belonged to the grimacing set who have visiting-cards, and are
> proud to be thought richer than their neighbours.' (XXVII, 41–2)

Personal interest in Felix Holt centres on the triangular situation
between Felix, Esther and Harold Transome, a rival radical. This
is paralleled in *Beauchamp's Career* by the relationship between
Beauchamp, Cecilia and Tuckham, Beauchamp's cousin.

Beauchamp's radicalism is sharply contrasted with Tuckham's
conservatism. The latter says to Cecilia: 'My aim for my country is
to have the land respected. For that purpose we must have power;
for power wealth; for wealth industry; for industry internal peace:
therefore no agitation, no artificial divisions. All's plain in history
and fact, so long as we do not obtrude sentimentalism. Nothing

mixes well with that stuff—except poetical ideas!' (XLVI, 529–30) The conflict between Beauchamp and Tuckham, which is demonstrated throughout the book, arises from their sharp differences in political attitude. Meredith is not tempted to develop a plot of intrigue over the question of inheritance, and Tuckham is instrumental in Beauchamp's receipt of a legacy from Mrs Beauchamp.

Between Felix and Harold, on the other hand, political differences are less marked: rather than honest intellectual disagreement, the conflict between them centres on their interest in Esther, which overshadows the political theme. Where Felix's radicalism is weak, Harold's is insincere. He sees in radicalism a means of attaining greater prosperity: 'The world of which Treby Magna was the centre was naturally curious to see the young Transome, who had come from the East, was as rich as a Jew, and called himself a Radical'. (XVIII, 288) As one native believes, he takes up with Radicals 'only to get into Parliament; he'll turn around when he gets there'. (XX, 311) His political career is related to egoism: 'I always meant to be an Englishman, and thrash a lord or two who thrashed me at Eton', he says. (I, 26)

Esther herself remains a conventional character all through her moral, rather than amorous, struggle. Her abandonment of Harold and Transome Court for Felix and his modest surroundings is arbitrary and not the outcome of significant change in her character or her politics. Felix influences Esther by preaching what Barbara Hardy calls 'transmutation of self'.[11] His pedagogic account of Byron, which seems to influence Esther, is in itself inconsistent with his own practice, for he is not free from the impact of Byronism whether expressed in his melancholy or in his final detachment from society. Esther cannot see this inconsistency nor can she argue about his views. She feels obliged 'to imagine what he would like her to be, and what sort of views he took of life so as to make it seem valuable in the absence of all elegance, luxury, gaiety, or romance'. (XV, 256) She is reduced to a conventional type of woman as she looks for the secret of the compromise: 'She knew that Felix cared earnestly for all public questions, and she supposed that he held it one of her deficiencies not to care about them: well, she would try to learn the secret of this ardour, which was so strong in him that it animated what she thought the dullest form of life.' (XVIII, 289)

Cecilia, on the other hand, is a character whose growth is demonstrated throughout the novel. She originally admires Beauchamp for his heroism in life-saving. She becomes vaguely

attracted to him when he emerges as political hero, but this
gradually puts her under trial.

In the early part of the involvement, Cecilia completely disap-
proves of Beauchamp's 'present adventure' in politics. She considers
it an obligation to try and 'cure him of his mental errors and
excesses'. As she tries to explain to herself Beauchamp's political
career (this is not the point of view we are invited to adopt), she
contemplates the possibility of his politics being motivated by 'a
lover's despair'. (xvii, 173) At this stage Beauchamp is a 'friend and
foe'. With the ordeal of conflict Cecilia's heroism (which can be
defined as the struggle of innovation against convention) gradually
emerges to present the most lively aspect of the tension in the book.

Unlike Esther, Cecilia does not accept Beauchamp all at once.
She admires him as an individual apart from his political views. She
assumes that Renée admires him equally for his individual style.
(xvii, 176) In canvassing, Cecilia dwells more on his individual
qualities such as competence in conversation and his command of
temper. This, she thinks, would make him liked among the poor.
Beauchamp 'is too much of a political mystic', she remarks to
Mr Austin. (xviii, 178)

The interaction between public and private life becomes more
intricate as the conflict grows to involve social circumstances.
Cecilia's opposition to Beauchamp's political views is not motivated
merely by her political conviction as a Tory, but more by the social
convention of the time concerning the upbringing of women. This
can be seen in the conversation between Cecilia and Mrs Lespel
when Cecilia says: 'The wife you would give him [Beauchamp]
should be a creature rooted in nothing—in sea-water'. (xx, 206)
Cecilia's desire to break from the established social order conflicts
with her fear of loss of security which this would entail.

In Meredith this fear is not presented merely as an aspect of social
realism (as it is in George Eliot's description of pathetic disability in
her female characters), but in the context of the conflict between the
old and the new, where a new sensibility struggles to emerge.
Meredith believes in courage as a positive power necessary for
change, whether in private or public life, and he often refers to
cowardice as the negative power which helps maintain the
established order.[12]

Cecilia, like her fellow female characters, is individualised, and
her conflict is internalised. It is more than a conflict between her
and Beauchamp. Her remark to Mrs Lespel obliquely implies that

she ought to come to terms wtih her fears of being uprooted before a reconciliation with Beauchamp can take place.

Beauchamp himself remarks in his early involvement with Renée that their partnership requires courage on her side, besides independence (from his uncle) on his own. At one time he sees the scheme as a failure because Renée lacks courage. He remarks that she dreads the risks of the scheme. (x, 90) Even to Jenny Denham, who has a background of radical politics, 'marrying Beauchamp was no simple adventure. She feared in her bosom, and resigned herself.' (LVI, 621)

The source of fear in the three female characters is related to Beauchamp's politics, which society as a whole dreads. Cecilia expresses her fear of Beauchamp's radicalism early in the book when she says: 'So you would blow up my poor Mount Laurels for a peace-offering to the lower classes?' Beauchamp replies 'I should hope to put it on a stronger foundation, Cecilia'. (XVII, 164) The resolution of conflict in Cecilia begins with the breakdown of these fears.

Change in Cecilia is not sudden. It is sometimes suspended by her hope that 'the madness of the pursuit of his political chimaera might change his character', (XXVII, 308) before she herself may face a final surrender. Nor does the change happen without discomfort, as we see, for example, in Cecilia's further conversation with Mrs Lespel. (xx, 206–7)

Cecilia reveals a significant change in her politics as she argues with Tuckham in Italy about the English middle-class family in Rome, Beauchamp and the poor, whom she believes have a cause to be pleaded. She becomes critical of England and the English. Tuckham's complacency contrasts with Cecilia's radical views, as he says to her that the world feels the power of the English and has confidence in their good faith. (XLVI, 528–9)

The relationship between Beauchamp and Cecilia reaches a climax when Cecilia is 'conquered' yet 'unclaimed' by her conqueror. The situation is given an effective description:

> The room she had looked to as a refuge from Nevil was now her stronghold against the man whom she had incredibly accepted. She remained there, the victim of a heart malady, under the term of headache. Feeling entrapped, she considered that she must have been encircled and betrayed. She looked back on herself as a giddy figure falling into a pit: and in the pit she lay. (XLVIII, 545)

Cecilia's vision of Beauchamp—where private and public sides of his career are seen in interaction—is presented in the paragraph which follows. Cecilia is tortured by the evolving vision of the new situation, as expressed in the monologue which follows. Attempting to overcome her dejection, she tries to rationalise the situation. She wants to believe that Beauchamp is no spiritual guide as she finds that her heart pleads for him. But this is only the negative side of her vision.

Beauchamp's departure from Mount Laurels finally brings about the end of the relationship. Beauchamp and Cecilia are, however, spiritually united. The union is enacted in imagery. Cecilia's state parallels the concluding situation of 'the insignificant bit of mudbank life remaining in this world in the place of [Beauchamp]', where she is left 'to sink into an agreeable stupor, like one deposited on a mudbank after buffeting the waves'. (XLVIII, 548)

She is symbolically saved by the life-saving hero whom she earlier admired. But she is saved to unite with him: 'The revelling libertine open sea wedded her to Beauchamp in that veiled cold spiritual manner she could muse on as a circumstance out of her life'. (XLVIII, 550)

Cecilia's development as a character illustrates the tribute to realism that is present in the novel. Meredith intervenes in the course of the narrative of the following paragraph which deals with this point: 'My way is like a Rhone island in the summer drought, stony, unattractive and difficult between the two forceful streams of the unreal and the over-real, which delight mankind—honour to the conjurors! My people conquer nothing, win none; they are actual, yet uncommon.' (XLVIII, 552–3) Meredith implies that writers can establish popularity by adopting the stream of the unreal—romance—or of the over-real—the kind of realism suggested in the tendency to portray facts and events with mimetic accuracy and transparent motivation. He is even more specific when he says: 'Those happy tales of mystery are as much my envy as the popular narratives of the deeds of bread and cheese people, for they both create a tide-way in the attentive mind'. (XLVIII, 552) Meredith shares the tendency of his contemporaries in reaction against romance and the sensational school,[13] but does not share their advocacy of the picture of 'our real-life acquaintance' as the highest achievement in the presentation of incident and character.[14] He is, for example, distinguished from Trollope, who saw the real 'somewhere between naturalism and complete artificiality',[15] and from George Eliot, who finds in the real a new forceful way of writing.[16] They identified the real with the common: but Meredith's 'real', to which he gives the term 'actual', is uncommon. Here Meredith is closer to the principle of selection in art and the tension between art and life than those of his contemporaries who, despite their concern with criticism, were unable to work out an elaborate 'theory of outright realism', as Kenneth Graham calls it.[17]

Critics of *Beauchamp's Career*, contemporary and modern, have focussed on Beauchamp's failures in politics, in personal life, in his death and, in general, as a hero. They have tended to overlook certain aspects of the novel, for example the interpolated critical paragraphs and the significance of the points of view of various characters, which illuminate the nature of Meredith's theme and character presentation.

Contemporary reviewers based their criticism on Beauchamp's failure as a Carlylean hero. The *Examiner* remarks that Beauchamp 'was of little avail in overturning the abuses of society'.[18] The *Pall Mall Gazette* similarly notices that 'the ultra-Radical young aristocrat, thrown upon a world socially and politically out of joint, and self-dedicated, like Hamlet, to a mission beyond his strength therein, Mr. Meredith has drawn for us one of those later Quixotes where fate is the more pathetic in that they tilt vainly at real giants, which only the rest of the world conspire to call windmills'.[19] This point is made also by the *British Quarterly Review*, which sees that Beauchamp lacks insight and has 'some moral deficiencies that partly account for his failure in "winning souls"'.[20]

The reviews acknowledge in Beauchamp the Carlylean element of insight which helps him to perceive 'truly what the time wanted', but they do not seem to accept his non-Carlylean inability to 'lead it on the right thither'.

Beauchamp's failure remains a target for modern critical dogma. Walter Wright, Norman Kelvin and V. S. Pritchett consider Beauchamp an impulsive egoist, and each views him within the framework of his general approach to Meredith.[21]

Wright considers Beauchamp's career 'composed of fragments, of things never quite completed'. Searching for the plot of action he comments: 'His career is not, of course, an orderly progress towards the gaining of wisdom. Rather it is perpetual adventure, with folly coming as well late as early and with prudence learned through mistakes being of little avail against new kinds of temptation to error.' Kelvin and Pritchett similarly argue that Beauchamp's action is distorted by impulsive commitments.

The three critics take the conflict as being in Beauchamp himself: to use their terms, between 'heart and head', 'the rational and irrational' or 'passion and duty'. This consequently leads to the under-estimation of the public side in the conflict. Wright dismisses in a casual summary of the novel Meredith's purpose as described in his letter (1, 485), and remarks that it 'is not at all complete and it minimises Beauchamp's adventure, but it indicates the author's conscious attempt to relate Beauchamp directly to the culture of the novelist's own age'. Thus he takes the book to be a romantic comedy of egoism and adventure. Kelvin, too, misrepresents the political aspects of the book in speaking of 'Meredith's conviction that political principles designed to produce a rational society can be used as an excuse for disastrously irrational behaviour'. Pritchett does not recognise the impact of politics on Beauchamp's life beyond the traditional consideration of duty versus passion.

In their moral evaluation of the resolution of plot the three critics find the ending lacking in heroism. Applying the traditional standards of romance and heroism to Beauchamp's action, Wright concludes that 'it is the unheroic rather than the sublime which has triumphed'. Kelvin's interpretation of Beauchamp's defeat is similar. He views the conclusion as a lack of compromise between the rational and irrational which, he thinks, brings about the triumph of the latter. He remarks that the form of presentation fails to accommodate the author's image of the rational man. Pritchett sees Beauchamp's marriage to Jenny as a 'brief dull' one and his death as a consequence of an 'ordeal and defeat'.

These critics have overlooked Meredith's plan to present heroism in the novel as a 'certain drama of self-conquest'. Meredith's critical message, interpolated as it is in the novel, does not seem to have reached or satisfied the reviewers, whose moral standard of judgement led them to focus on failure as a consequence of weakness in his character.

Towards a contribution for a unified plan Meredith also undertakes to justify Beauchamp's failure in politics. This is carried out from the various points of view in the book. Rosamund's stands for that of the common reader, when she tells Romfrey of her feeling that 'our Nevil!—has accomplished hardly anything, if anything!' Romfrey counters this point of view when he replies: 'No: we haven't had much public excitement out of him. But one thing he did do: *he got me down on my knees!*' The narrative continues: 'Lord Romfrey pronounced these words with a sober emphasis that struck the humour of it sharply into Rosamund's heart, through some contrast it presented between Nevil's aim at the world and hit of a man: the immense deal thought of it by the earl, and the very little that Nevil would think of it—the great domestic achievement to be boasted of by an enthusiastic devotee of politics!' (LV, 616) Romfrey's conclusion recalls Shrapnel's reaction to the loss of the election when he says to Lydiard: 'Note, then, that Radicals, always marching to the triumph, never taste it; and for Tories it is Dead Sea fruit, ashes in their mouths! Those Liberals, those temporisers, compromisers, a concourse of atoms! glorify themselves in the animal satisfaction of sucking the juice of the fruit, for which they pay with their souls. They have no true cohesion, for they have no vital principle.' (XXVII, 294) Beauchamp's comment on the election is reported: 'It's only a skirmish lost, and that counts for nothing in a battle without end: it must be incessant.' (XXVII, 296) His hope of a long revolution is further revealed when he muses: 'Ghastly as a minority is in an Election, in a lifelong struggle it is refreshing and encouraging. The young world and its triumph is with the minority.' (XXXVIII, 427) Meredith expresses the same view in an unpublished extract from his *Notebook*.

A Radical Philosopher to a Root Tory:
'If we capture from you one fool in a century and transform him, it is the utmost of our expectation. You Sir, we shall fail to catch, and your son perhaps and your grandson: we may never have one of your family. But our one will be found elsewhere in a hundred years. We feel that we may say we are certain of him: and on such a prediction do we base our hope.'[22]

Jack Lindsay is the critic of Meredith who deals most seriously with politics in *Beauchamp's Career*. His criticism is, however, as limited as that of others by the dogmatic presuppositions with which he approaches the book. His analysis is based on the theory of class struggle: 'Every time Beauchamp could cash in on a situation, like other members of his class, he further detaches himself. Morally and politically, he ascends; from the point of view of his class, he goes down.'[23]

Though Beauchamp is born in the upper class, he develops different connections and beliefs. He antagonises his uncle as soon as he realises that his radicalism and his uncle's opportunism in politics are irreconcilable. He marries Jenny, 'of whose birth and blood we know nothing,' Rosamund says, lamenting his loss of Cecilia. (LV, 615) His criticism of Rosamund marrying above her rank is not, I think, motivated by his class consciousness, as Lindsay takes it, but rather by his contempt of Rosamund, who accepts his uncle simply because she is weak and feels inferior to him. When Colonel Halkett warns Beauchamp against the result of the election with the intention of instructing him that 'a man owes a duty to his class', Beauchamp replies: 'A man owes a duty to his class as long as he sees his class doing its duty to the country'. (XVI, 161) Radicalism in Beauchamp is strong enough to make him transcend the values and beliefs of his class, and the simple pleasures he is occasionally seen to enjoy, such as that of the yacht, are too casual and insignificant to affect his radical stand. At the same time, it individualises Beauchamp's character. The early picture of *Beauchamp's Career*, where Lindsay finds his demonstration, mainly serves as a background from which a later different career evolves. It is Meredith's practice to provide such background, as he does later in *One of Our Conquerors*, where he presents Victor's early life in the first chapter of the book and by which Lindsay is similarly misled in his judgement of Victor's character.

Lindsay ascribes the limitation in Meredith's politics to his reliance on his friend Maxse, who is undoubtedly the model for Beauchamp, assuming that neither Maxse nor Hyndman (the model for Victor) knew enough socialism to help Meredith grasp the nature of class-State. He comments that 'the only serious flaw in his political ideas' is that Meredith 'never got fully clear the nature and function of the class-State, though at moments his definition is accurate enough. He remains unstable at this point because he did not move on to find his place in an organised working-class with its party seeking always to unify theory and practice, and always fundamentally opposed to the class-State. Hence he wobbles from a powerful statement of the class-struggle as the sole key to progress into reconciliation-formulas that can only work out as betraying progress—"national unity" in "defence" of ill-gotten gains.'[24]

Lindsay inaccurately takes some of Shrapnel's eloquence and Beauchamp's speech to suggest 'reconciliation formulas', Utopian theories, or ideals of peace. But the politics of the time were not so specific in their technicality, and it was not unusual for talk about humanity in general to involve national or even local affairs. Maxse, for example, uses one to mean the other when he talks about 'National Education': 'Surely it must be done by a common universal machinery—that is to say, by a national system.'[25] Neither for Shrapnel nor for Beauchamp will politics mean Disraeli's 'national unity' or Gladstone's 'international league'— two signs of the betrayal of progress. At the same time, the 'national unity in defence' which Beauchamp talks about in his early career is overwhelmed by other major political issues which evolve with the progress of his career, and it is not elaborated to a significant degree.

The criticism that Beauchamp and Shrapnel fail to put theory into practice is invalidated by the purpose of the book and its actual historical circumstances. There would be no tension between the ideal of character and the reality of society if the two politicians were to succeed, as both would be transformed into one reality, where the conflict between the idealism of art and the reality of the time disappears. It would consequently become a political or social thesis fit for a new successful Carlylean hero. For Meredith it would mean a way of moralising which he deliberately avoids both in *Beauchamp's Career* and in *Harry Richmond*.[26] The point of 'the need of men like Shrapnel or Beauchamp to advance from the theory of fellowship to the full union of theory and practice' is outside Meredith's purpose. He sees that his characters are neither winners nor conquerors even if they are fighters in society.

Lindsay imposes on the book a purpose of his own when he comments that 'Meredith is clear enough to see what is holding Beauchamp (Maxse) back, but he cannot realise what will liberate him into effectiveness'.[27] As it is Meredith's main concern to present the circumstances of Beauchamp's struggle against the conditions of the time—in an emotional outcry, he says to Rosamund, 'Stones are easier to move than your English' (XLII, 471)—it is left to the reader to see what would liberate him into effectiveness.[28] Beauchamp transcends the condition of the time through the survival of his revolutionary vision. His career is subject to the conditions of the time, and achievements of its theme.

Beauchamp's Career ends in the drowning incident and the comment exchanged in silence between Dr Shrapnel and Lord Romfrey remains suggestive of various interpretations. Reviewers reacted vigorously to Beauchamp's death,[29] and the general tendency among commentators is to consider it symbolic of Beauchamp's self-denial and sacrifice for the public cause. This is not, I think, all that it implies.

The fact that the silent comment is shared by Lord Romfrey and Dr Shrapnel is significant: 'That is what we have in exchange for Beauchamp! It was not uttered, but it was visible in the blank stare at one another of the two men who loved Beauchamp, after they had examined the insignificant bit of mudbank life remaining in this world in the place of him.' The pronoun 'we' is relevant if not specifically referring to the country which denied Beauchamp throughout his career 'a conceivable epic'. The reactionary peer unites with the radical Doctor in his awareness of the country's loss of Beauchamp. On the part of Lord Romfrey, the realisation recalls and confirms his confession to Rosamund of Beauchamp's influence on him in soliciting the apology for Dr Shrapnel.

The joint response further suggests his acknowledgement of the element of right in the revolutionary principle—in itself a victory for Beauchamp and his spiritual guide. It equally implies a victory for Beauchamp's heroism—being a revelation and an influence, and not an accomplished action. It is symbolic, I think, that the spirit of revolution (Shrapnel) survives the death of its bearer (Beauchamp).

Beauchamp's failure and death demonstrate, from a comparative point of view, how Meredith succeeds while Carlyle fails to question what A. J. LaValley describes as 'the formal indestructibility of hero-worship and the somewhat facile alliance of hero-worship with the external law of the world'.[30] It similarly distinguishes Meredith's consistent vision from Carlyle's paradoxical vision of heroism and revolution, in that the future is viewed as a continuation of the present, whereas Carlyle has to accept the future flowing from the past, the present being problematic.

Commentators who resent Beauchamp's death have probably not realised that a reconciliation to life may seem superfluous, at least to Meredith, who kept the tragic end as it is despite the reviewers' and his wife's revolt against it. Unlike Vittoria, Beauchamp cannot be reconciled to history because history in *Beauchamp's Career* is not a single battle, but a continuous struggle which has not ended. Marriage may not be considered as a means of reconciliation as in *Harry Richmond*, because the conflict is mainly between him and the antagonist society, and not in himself.

Beauchamp's death is, like Richard's, undoubtedly painful, but unlike Richard's it is allied with the survival of a vision which transcends physical time. Richard dies 'blind', but Beauchamp, like his model, dies with a vision. In this connection Meredith's comment to Clodd is apt: 'Sometimes *Harry Richmond* is my favourite, but I am inclined to give the palm to *Beauchamp's Career*. There is a breezy, human interest about it; and the plot has a consistency and logical evolution which *Feverel* lacks . . . I miss the Admiral [Maxse] very much, but he who has looked through life has also looked through death.'[31]

It is worthwhile, moreover, to remember that Beauchamp leaves a son behind to look through life.

5 *One of Our Conquerors*: Deeper Dimension

As in *Beauchamp's Career*, Meredith concerns himself with the history of the time. Writing to Augustus Jessop (May 1890) he says: 'I have condemned myself both to a broad and a close observation of the modern world in it,—throwing beams both upon its rat-tides and its upper streamers' (II, 999). Commenting on the harsh reception of *One of Our Conquerors* Meredith reiterates this observation and writes (June 1890): 'What they call digressions, is a presentation of the atmosphere of the present time, of which the story issues'. (II, 1034)

The 'broad observation of the modern world' and the 'presentation of the atmosphere of the present time' are two phrases descriptive of the topicality of the novel (typicality of character) out of which emerges the individuality of character referred to as 'close observation'. 'Broad' and 'close' are two key words referring to public and private life, and as in *Beauchamp's Career* the portrayal of character is presented by means of the interplay of the two.

The milieu of *One of Our Conquerors* is the late 1880s, but the narrative frequently moves back to the earlier years of the century and occasionally forward towards the nineties. It can be located in the expanding England described by Tennyson in his *An Ode in Honour of the Jubilee of Queen Victoria*:

> Fifty years of ever-broadening Commerce!
> Fifty years of ever-brightening Science!
> Fifty years of ever-widening Empire![1]

A detailed picture of the Victorian England which forms a background for *One of Our Conquerors* occurs in H. G. Wells:

> Upon the surface and in its general structure that British world of the eighties had a delusive air of final establishment. Queen Victoria had been reigning for close upon half a century and

seemed likely to reign for ever. The economic system of unrestricted private enterprise with privately owned capital had yielded a great harvest of material prosperity, and few people suspected how rapidly it was exhausting the soil of willing service in which it grew. . . . Wars went on, a marginal stimulation of the empire, but since the collapse of Napoleon I no war had happened to frighten England for its existence as a country; no threat of warfare that could touch English life or English soil troubled men's imagination. Ruskin and Carlyle had criticised English ideals and the righteousness of English commerce and industrialism, but they were regarded generally as eccentric and unaccountable men . . . ; a certain amount of trade competition from the United States and from other European countries was developing, but at most it ruffled the surface of the national self-confidence. There was a socialist movement, but it was still only a passionless criticism of trade and manufacturers, a criticism poised between aesthetic fastidiousness and benevolence.

Wells then goes on to describe the gradual fall of the old gods and the rise of self-criticism in place of complacency:

The fifty-year old faith on which the social and political fabric rested—for all social and political fabrics must in the last resort rest upon faith—was being corroded and dissolved and removed. Britain in the mid-Victorian time stood strong and sturdy in the world because a great number of its people, its officials, employers, professional men and workers honestly believed in the rightness of its claims and professions. . . . But from the middle of the century onward this assurance of the prosperous British in their world was being subjected to a more and more destructive criticism, spreading slowly from intellectual circles into the general consciousness.[2]

It is the same England A. Vizetelly describes in his Preface to the English translation of Zola's *L'Argent*: 'And with regard to this English version, it may, I think, be safely said that its publication is well timed, for the rottenness of our financial world has become such a crying scandal, and the inefficiency of our company laws has been so fully demonstrated, that the absolute urgency of reform can no longer be denied'.[3]

Contemporary writers like W. E. Henley, W. T. Stead and

Rudyard Kipling were fascinated by the affairs of the Empire and its political background. Meredith found the political scene of the eighties distressing. He wrote to George Stevenson (April 1887): 'We Liberals, Radicals, practical Christians, are going through a gloomy time. Politics, even when they have us in thorniest thickets, do not obscure me. I see under the edge of the cloudiest. But it is nevertheless distressing to observe one's countrymen bemuddled by their alarms and selfish temporary interests.'4 (II, 858) The England of the eighties was evidently a 'darkest England' for him, but he did not subscribe to the various middle class reformist solutions, such as Booth's Salvation Army (his *Darkest England and the Way Out* appeared at approximately the same time as the novel) or other efforts to improve the situation of the poor. In a letter in E. M. Forster's papers, Meredith writes to Miss Forster (November 1889): 'You touch on our differences in politics: but when women of our easier classes descend among the poor to interest and lift them, they do more than radicals for winning heaven's blessings on an otherwise unrighteous order of things. Would that there were more of you!—the present Structure might then be preserved and our development to a sound brotherhood advance without a shock.'5

The picture of such a 'present structure' occurs in the first chapter of *One of Our Conquerors*. It comes to us refracted through the fears of Inchling (a successful entrepreneur) which precipitate Victor's own. Influenced by Inchling, Victor dreads the dominance of foreign commercial powers. His feelings are, however, fundamentally egoistic, for the England which he desires to see dominating the world is an extension of himself; and the title of an unpublished earlier draft of the book (*A Conqueror of Our Time*) is suggestive of this.6 Here Victor's portrait is more complex in its structure than Beauchamp's. While Beauchamp stands (with the ideal in him) against the England of which he is not a part, Victor intends to do so against the England of which he is an extension. In Beauchamp the conflict is between the internal and the external, but in Victor it is all internal.

The expansion of imperialism is the answer to Inchling's fears. In the eighties the notion of integrating the Empire into England was made popular by imperialists such as Sir John Seely, whose *Expansion of England* (1883) sold 80,000 copies within two years. The writer claimed that the Empire (with the exception of India) was a vast English nation. It is in this context that the opening in 1884 of the Empire Theatre, Leicester Square, and Florence Nightingale's call for a reprinting of Sir William Hunter's *Indian Empire* should be seen. The centre of this milieu is cosmopolitan London which towards the end of the century became a source of attraction for various writers as demonstrated in works like Crackanthorpe's *Battledore and Shuttlecock*, Street's *Episodes*, Egerton's *Discords and Keynotes*, Binyon's *London Visions* and Davidson's *Fleet Street Ecologues*. *One of Our Conquerors* is the only one of Meredith's novels where London is the main scene of action. Indeed, the ways in which the London scene is integrated in the consciousness of the characters becomes in this novel a major means towards their portrayal and that of the 'picture of the time'. This is demonstrated by the episode where the Rajah walking Eastward in the morning and Westward in the evening observes the 'belly-God' of England.[7] When the Rajah and his Minister go back to their own country, the narrative records, 'they speak of the hatted sect, which is most, or most commercially, succoured and fattened by our rule there'. (v, 37)

Out of this darkest England (where the broad observation lies) emerges the story of Victor's conquest. By the time the action of the book starts Victor is already a conqueror in the world of commercial power. He is a city millionaire. Behind him lies the career of the rising entrepreneur of the nineteenth century. But Victor is not a type of the Mammonism of his time. He is different from Zola's scheming financier, Saccard, the manager of the Universal Bank, who is always preoccupied with increasing his wealth and power. He is also different from Nicholas Forsyte in *The Man of Property*, who like Cecil Rhodes is prepared to make any sacrifice to support and maintain the Empire. The difference lies mainly in the internal conflict he experiences while trying to find a way out of the darkest England of which he is inevitably a product. However, he does not become a Marxist saviour like Zola's Sigismond Busch, whom Zola designs to contrast with Saccard. Victor is a comparatively more complex character for he attempts to fight against the thing which he dreads, but, at the same time, practises. Out of this conflict between the two sides of Victor, Meredith achieves a deeper penetration into the interplay between character and the conditions of the time.

The nature of the conflict in *One of Our Conquerors* illustrates Meredith's special emphasis on inner action as a means of character presentation. It has a narrower range of action than *Harry Richmond* whose concern is with the action of minds as well as fortune. In comparison with *Beauchamp's Career* it lacks plot. This characteristic recalls Henry James's letter to Compton Mackenzie:

> What the author shall do with his idea I am quite ready to wait for, but am meanwhile in no relation to the work at all unless that basis has been provided. Console yourself, however: dear great George Meredith once began to express what a novel he had just started ('One of our Conquerors') was to be about by no other art than by simply naming to me the half-dozen occurrences, such as they were, that occupied the pages he had already written; so that I remained, I felt, quite without any answer to my respectful inquiry—which he had all the time the very attitude of kindly encouraging and rewarding![8]

The action of the novel falls between two successive Aprils. Time is very much compressed, and while internal action expands, external action contracts. The first eleven chapters cover the incidents of the first two days. It is not likely that James would have gained much more even had Meredith introduced more incidents and written more pages. Victor, one imagines, would still be on London Bridge.

Victor is the man of 'punctilio' (a mode of expression he realises from the working-class man to be suggestive of his status as a man of wealth) who falls and consequently receives the Idea. He is punctilio, fall and Idea. Here Meredith uses a minimum of language condensed to convey a maximum of inner action. He touches on the eternal problem of language as a means of communication which was for him a perennial issue.[9] *One of Our Conquerors* expresses Meredith's awareness of the tension between art and life. It demonstrates Arthur Symons's remark that Meredith 'has intellectual passions for words, but has never been able to accustom his mind to the slowness of their service.'[10]

Meredith emphasises the connection between form and content by establishing a contrast between two groups of characters, implying that a wrong attitude to life inevitably leads to a distorted way of expressing its reality. One group comprises Dudley Sowerby who 'had in him just something more than is within the compass of the language of the meat-markets' (xxvi, 314); Colney Durance, with his 'pretentious and laboured Satiric Prose Epic of "THE RIVAL TONGUES"' (xxxvi, 432); Simeon Fenellan, who is 'a man of lean narrative, fit to chronicle political party wrangles and such like crop of carcase prose' (xxxvii, 438); and Mrs Burman who is nourished by comfortable fiction (xxxix, 478). In opposition to this group are Dartrey Fenellan, Nataly and Nesta. One group stands for the tradition of established order and the other for the dream of change. Meredith's terms for the two sides are Circumstances and Nature, and the conflict between them is what shapes Victor's life. It is the presentation of this conflict and not its resolution which is the concern of the book. The narrative wastes no time in presenting internal action. Victor's consciousness comes to us through the opening incident of the book. Victor falls down on London Bridge—the bridge of the city which he conquers—to awake from the intoxicating power of wealth. He is helped by a working-class man who surprises him with his reply to his 'amiable remonstrance': ' "And none of your dam punctilio," said the man'. (i, 3) Victor becomes disenchanted with the world of 'punctilio' which forms the basis of his life and alienates him from his fellow men. The man leaves him with the feeling of damnation by his own 'punctilio'.

Fall and damnation prompt the quest for salvation which comes to Victor in the form of a complex feeling referred to throughout the book as the 'Idea'. After the fall Victor chases the Idea which by no means in the book can be got hold of in time to save him. In presenting Victor's mind in action, Meredith uses devices which are very close to what in later criticism came to be known as the 'stream of consciousness' and, as the discussion of music later on demonstrates, 'objective correlative'. A detailed discussion of such devices and their relevance to the total structure of theme and character can bring us close to the nature of the author's achievement.

Action in the novel is carried forward by anxiety to attain the Idea and backward by fears aroused by the fall. This explains the slowness of action of which Meredith himself was aware as the beginning of Chapter ii shows.

Victor reflects on the fears which haunt him as a result of the fall: he feels shame and attributes this 'to the morbid indulgence in reflection: a disease never afflicting him anterior to the stupid fall on London Bridge. He rubbed instinctively for the punctilio-bump, and could cheat his fancy to think a remainder of it there. . . . He knew well it was fancy. But it was a fact also, that since the day of the fall (never, save in merest glimpses, before that day), he had taken to look behind him, as though an eye had been knocked in the back of his head.' (xviii, 191–2)

This morbid indulgence in reflection is well demonstrated in the scene in Chapter xiii where Victor recalls an incident that occurred in Chapter iii. Victor was thoughtlessly about to enter a chemist's shop frequently visited by Mrs Burman. His recollection of this incident is refracted through his dread of Mrs Burman as he says to Fenellan: '. . . when—I'm stating a fact—I distinctly—I'm sure of the shop—felt myself plucked back by the elbow; pulled back: the kind of pull when you have to put a foot backward to keep your equilibrium'.(xiii, 132–3) The panic in Victor is the outcome of a complex feeling of fear which combines his dread both of the fall and of Mrs Burman.

Another fear created by the fall concerns Victor's material and social success. The narrative recounts Victor's conviction, while on London Bridge, that the Law is 'and must ever be, the Law of the stronger'. Victor dreads losing the power of conquest which links him to society for fear of becoming 'food for lion and jackal'. His success, and Nataly's worship of 'the figure of success' in him, forms a link between them, arising as it does from her position as an individual deprived of social power in her own right through being a woman and an outcast. Victor is the only person who stands with her against the world; and this stance is made possible, to a large extent, by his success. Fear for their relationship is therefore implicit in Victor's fears for the successful continuance of his career: 'For, strange to confess, ever since the fall on London Bridge, his heart, influenced in some degree by Nataly's depression perhaps, had been shadowed by doubts of his infallible instinct for success'. (xxi, 255)

Thus the fall aroused in Victor an urgent awareness of the conflict inherent in his pursuit of public and private life, and the Idea appears to be the solution. It represents a means of achieving the ideal of reconciling society to nature.[11] It is not clearly defined and Victor struggles to bring it into consciousness. The monologue during his London walk shows him a means of putting into practice his dreams of becoming a public benefactor 'on the model of the hospitable Paduan'. The monologue is interrupted by the narrator's comment, emphasising Victor's sincerity: 'Dreams of this kind are taken at times by wealthy people as a cordial at the bar of benevolent intentions. But Victor was not the man to steal his refreshments in that known style. He meant to make deeds of them, as far as he could, considering their immense extension; and except for the sensitive social name, he was of single-minded purpose.' (v, 43) The narrative continues, introducing the scene in the chemist's shop, producing complex feelings about the fall, 'punctilio' and the Idea.

The Idea is brought close to Victor through Nesta: 'He began, under the influence of Nesta's companionship, to see the Goddess Nature there is in a chastened nature. And this view shook the curtain covering his lost Idea.' (xxxvi, 435) Nesta represents Nature and Victor's connection with it, while Mrs Burman is the symbol *par excellence* of society and Victor's link with it. As Nesta brings the Idea closer, Mrs Burman is felt to delay its realisation. Victor feels it is her mysteriously delayed death that keeps him 'crossing a bridge having a slippery bit on it'. (xxxvi, 435) Earlier he pleads she is on the side of

the enemy of Nature. —Tell us how? She is the slave of existing conventions. —And from what cause? She is the artificial production of a state that exalts her so long as she sacrifices daily and hourly to the artificial.

Therefore she sides with Mrs. Burman—the foe of Nature: who, with her arts and gold lures, has now possession of the Law (the brass idol worshipped by the collective) to drive Nature into desolation. (xiii, 137–8)

The contrast between nature and society is further worked out in other characters of the novel, who expose their acceptance or rejection of society in varying degrees. Carling, the lawyer, for example, believes that society is wrong, but accepts its morality because it exists. Inchling, the entrepreneur, is an extension of society. There is no conflict in him. Dudley finds it difficult to accept Nesta's origin despite the fact that 'his readings in modern books on heredity, pure blood, physical regeneration, pronounced approval of Nesta Radnor: and thereupon instinct opened mouth to speak; and a lockjaw seized it under that scowl of his presiding mistrust of Nature.' (xxxv, 420) On the other hand, Victor, Nataly, Nesta and Dartrey Fenellan share in the Idea: they are on the side of nature. Their capacity for the realisation of the Idea, however, varies.

Victor is unable to realise the Idea as long as he fails to free himself from his entanglement with society. Being 'desperately tempted by his never failing' (xxx, 360), he schemes to conquer society through material power and influence. The Lakelands venture, Victor's desire to secure Nesta's future in society through a socially acceptable marriage, and his standing for election to Parliament, fail to bring him closer to the Idea, and even obscure it because of their complicity with the values of a society which must be changed if the Idea is to be realised. It is important that Victor fell when he was thinking of 'the unfolding of the secret' of his Lakelands scheme to Nataly. The fall is closely associated, then, with the temptation of society.

Victor yields to this temptation not because he attaches more importance to his role in English society and to England's place in the Empire than to his personal and immediate relationships, but because his ideal is directed towards solving the conflict between them. Partially alienated as he is by living with Nataly, he still regards himself as 'the reverse of lawless; he inclined altogether towards good citizenship'. (XIII, 137) He does not accept the possibility of withdrawing from society as a solution, nor does he believe in anarchy as a means of change for 'he is too social to be captain of the socially insurgent'. (XIII, 138)

At one time Victor voices the notion, which we are not invited to accept, that he would be able to succeed if Nataly were more courageous: 'Then he would have been ready to teach the world that Nature—*honest* Nature—is more to be prized than Convention: a new Æra might begin'. (XIII, 138) Critics who accept weakness in Nataly as a source of inaction in the novel overlook the fact that choice for her is not less difficult than for Victor.[12] Having given him her life, she is tortured by the deception involved in being thought his wife. She shrinks from the prospect of living in Lakelands in those circumstances, but accepts the humiliation which Victor's pursuit of public life involves for herself. However, where Nesta is concerned, she takes action to prevent her daughter becoming entangled at the expense of truth in a socially advantageous marriage, in accordance with Victor's schemes, to Dudley Sowerby; she envisages the possibility of Nesta's marriage to Dartrey Fenellan. While Nataly is silent, Nesta voices her mother's distress about the maintenance of the deception. She says to Victor as they plan a day to explore the prospective site for Lakelands: 'To go and see the nest? Only, please, not a big one. A real nest; where mama and I can wear dairymaid's hat and apron all day—the style you like; and strike roots. We've been torn away two or three times: twice, I know.' (VI, 48)

Nesta and Dartrey emerge as the emblem of the new era. Nesta stands mid-way between Diana and Carinthia, both of whom present a more elaborate picture of the new anti-establishment woman. Dartrey resembles Woodseer in *The Amazing Marriage*. Nesta and Dartrey are free to be effective in action on the side of nature, but the picture of the new era is not fully developed in the present novel where the emphasis is on the conflict in the transition from the old to the new order as it is seen in Victor and Nataly. This brings us to the nature of the conflict and its mode of expression.

Conflict in *One of Our Conquerors* centres on Victor's struggle to bring the Idea into consciousness, and to overcome the distressing feelings aroused by the fall, bringing as it does 'morbid reflection' about the past and the present. Because these feelings are painful, Victor would prefer to forget them and shrinks from revealing them. Meredith attacks modern realists in fiction for their claim to present a credible portrait of human nature by means of strictly 'factual' and detailed reporting. (XIII, 130) Equally he attacks 'lean narrative' writers for their belief that truth can be revealed through rendering a factual account of incidents in sequential order. An alternative approach to these two tendencies is seen in the novel where the characters' inclination to suppress rather than express the truth of situations is explored. Interior monologue and what can be identified as the 'stream of consciousness' become the appropriate form for rendering character consciousness where action is presented as unspoken suffering.

After Victor regains his balance from the fall he refuses 'to feel any sensible bruise on his head, with the admission that he perhaps might think he felt one: which was virtually no more than the feeling of a thought'. (II, 14) Victor avoids defining his feelings in order that they may not become a thought, and consequently an established fact. He similarly rejects the feelings of misfortune which come to his mind at random after the fall: 'We do not speak of them: we have not words to stamp the indefinite things; generally we should leave them unspoken if we had the words; we know them as out of reason: they haunt us, pluck at us, fret us, nevertheless'. (IV, 34) Reviewing his past Victor reflects on his involvement with Mrs Burman: 'Can we really loathe the first of the steps when the one in due sequence, cousin to it, is a blessedness? If we have been righted to health by a medical draught, we are bound to be respectful to our drug. And so we are, in spite of Nature's wry face and shiver at a mention of what

we went through during those days, those horrible days:—hide
them!' (v, 46).

With Nataly, Victor is evasive about painful issues, and she too is
reluctant to express them. As he talks to Nataly about the
Lakelands' project, she finds it strange that Victor, 'of the most
quivering sensitiveness on her behalf, could not see, that he threw
her into situations where hard words of men and women threatened
about her head; where one or two might on a day, some day, be
heard; and where, in the recollection of two years back, the word
"Impostor" had smacked her on both cheeks from her own mouth'.
(vi, 52) In the course of discussing the furnishing of the new house,
Nataly hints at her preference for a cottage, but Victor in an evasive
allusion to the *Arabian Nights*, implying the sense of his own
infallibility and producing a situation of romance and comedy,
prevents a direct revelation of the truth as he knows it. (vi, 53) Both
Victor and Nataly shrink from referring to Mrs Burman and issues
related to her. A monologue describes Victor's jealousy of Dartrey
as a result of the death of his wife:

> Dartrey free, he was relieved of the murderous drama
> incessantly in the mind of the shackled men.
> It seemed like one of the miracles of a divine intervention, that
> Dartrey should be free, suddenly free; and free while still a
> youngish man. He was in himself a wonderful fellow, the pick of
> his country for vigour, gallantry, trustiness, high-mindedness; his
> heavenly good fortune decked him as a prodigy.' (iv, 34)

Victor does not tell Nataly of Dartrey's widowhood, 'for a
downright dread of renewing his painful fit of envy'. (vi, 57)

As news is received that Mrs Burman's death is imminent (xvi,
173–4) her haunting image intensifies the alienation between
Nataly and Victor: 'And between him and that dear woman, since
the communication made by Skepsey in the town of Dreux, nightly
the dividing spirit of Mrs Burman lay: cold as a corpse. They both
felt her there. They kissed coldly, pressed a hand, said good night.'
(xviii, 197) Later in the novel, this recurs in a more violent and
dramatic form:

> Victor smartly commended her to slumber, with heaven's
> blessing on her and a dose of soft nursery prattle.
> He squeezed her hand. He kissed her lips by day. She heard

him sigh settling himself into the breast of night for milk of sleep, like one of the world's good children. She could have turned to him, to show him she was in harmony with the holy night and loving world, but for the fear founded on a knowledge of the man he was; it held her frozen to the semblance of a tombstone lady beside her lord, in the aisle where horror kindles pitchy blackness with its legions at one movement. Verily it was the ghost of Mrs. Burman come to the bed, between them. (xx, 225)

Both continue to feel 'the power of Mrs. Burman to put division between them': their speculations about it remain unformulated. (xxii, 268)

The painful issues which cause disruption between Nataly and Victor arise from the fact that their relationship exists in defiance of society. While they wait for the opportunity to justify their relationship in the eyes of society through marriage, they conceal their lawless state from society. The suffering caused by this concealment to Nataly is felt throughout the book, and particularly in Chapter xxx where Nataly reveals to Dartrey her daily ordeal. Victor justifies the concealment in Chapter xiii:

He pleaded his case in their [the heavens'] accustomed hearing:— a youngster tempted by wealth, attracted, besought, snared, revolted, etc. And Mrs. Burman, when roused to jealousy, had shown it by teazing him for a confession of his admiration of splendid points in the beautiful Nataly, the priceless fair woman living under their roof, a contrast of very life with the corpse and shroud; and she seen by him daily, singing with him, her breath about him, her voice incessantly upon every chord of his being!

He pleaded successfully. But the silence following the verdict was heavy; the silence contained an unheard thunder. It was the sound, as when out of Court the public is dissatisfied with a verdict. (xiii, 137)

Victor pleads that he is justified in flouting the laws of society in order to keep faith with nature. Society does not admit nature as evidence. There is therefore no possibility of communication and to speak of 'the torments of those days of the monstrous alliance' to men, is futile.

Music functions in the novel as 'the liberating alternative to language'.[13] Where language falls short of accommodating the dilemma of character, music tempers the conflict between communication and silence.

Meredith used music in his previous works, but mainly as a theme or symbol. In *Emilia in England* and *Vittoria* the heroine is an opera singer, who makes of singing both a career and a symbolic gesture. Beauchamp says to Jenny Denham that music makes him think. In *Diana of the Crossways* the title of the opera 'I Puritani' is suggestive of the ironical situation between Diana and Dacier. But in *One of Our Conquerors* music is an integral part of character experience which articulates consciousness and situation.

Victor and Nataly sang together at Mrs Burman's house, and their love was born of this union. For them and their Nesta music brings about the harmony of the family: 'Nesta's promising soprano, and her mother's contralto, and his baritone—a true baritone, not so well trained as their accurate notes—should be rising in spirited union with the curtain of that secret: there was matter for song and concert, triumph and gratulation in it.' (II, 14) When Victor and Nataly entertain, they do so through musical parties as music provides a subject and a medium to link them with society without involving situations which may reveal the truth.

Music stands between Victor and his dilemma: 'He sang: he never acknowledged a trouble, he dispersed it'. (VI, 50) It is opera that Victor enjoys and his taste is for 'the old barleysugar of Bellini or a Donizetti-Serenade'. His first opera was 'La Sonnambula', of which he says to Fenellan that 'it would task the highest poetry— say, require, if you like—showing all that's noblest, splendidest, in a young man, to describe its effect on me'. (XIII, 139) He deplores the influence of Wagner on the later compositions of Verdi and Gounod:

'I trace him in Gounod's Romeo et Juliette—and we don't gain by it; we have a poor remuneration for the melody gone; think of the little shepherd's pipeing in *Mireille*; and there's another in *Sapho*—delicious. I held out against Wagner as long as I could. The Italians don't much more than Wagnerize in exchange for the loss of melody. They would be wiser in going back to Pergolese, Campagnole. The *Mefistofile* was good—of the school of the foreign master. *Aida* and *Otello*, no.' (XIII, 139)

It is in early opera, in its emphasis on melody and sentiment that Victor can forget his troubles. He is 'seduced by cadences'. His description of Wagner's 'tap of his pedagogue's baton' suggests that he finds in the more complex and emotionally demanding music of Wagner experiences into which he does not wish to enter: in the tension of this music he finds his own tensions reflected. He searches in music that which suspends rather than that which reflects his situation: it functions as an 'objective correlative' for his feelings: 'Victor hinted notes of the Conspiration Scene closing the Third Act of the *Huguenots*. That sombre Chorus brought Mrs. Burman before him. He drummed the *Rataplan*, which sent her flying.' (XIII, 140)

While music provides a refuge from suffering that language cannot provide, it cannot offer a solution. The solution is the attainment of the Idea. Just as language is inadequate to express suffering, it is inadequate to express the Idea.

Throughout the book the Idea is aroused in Victor's mind by associations. This is demonstrated in the morbid scene when Victor and Nataly pass Regent's Park Zoo on their way to visit Mrs Burman: ' "After all, a caged wild beast hasn't so bad a life," he said. —To be well fed while they live, and welcome death as a release from the maladies they develop in idleness, is the condition of wealthy people:—creatures of prey? horrible thought! yet allied to his Idea, it seemed.' (XL, 484) In incidents such as this, Victor feels that his Idea is close, but when put into words it is reduced in stature: 'He fell to work at Nataly's "aristocracy of the contempt of luxury"; signifying, that we the wealthy will not exist to pamper flesh, but we live for the promotion of brotherhood:—ay, and that our England must make some great moral stand, if she is not to fall to the rear and down. Unuttered, it caught the skirts of the Idea: it evaporated when spoken.' (XL, 485) Such incidents occur with increasing frequency towards the end of the book. Victor's monologue becomes evermore tense as the death of Mrs Burman draws close. The narrative of his thoughts as he wakes on the morning of his great undelivered speech reviews all the elements of his conflict:

His lost Idea drew close to him in sleep: or he thought so, when awaking to the conception of a people solidified, rich and poor, by the common pride of simple manhood. But it was not coloured, not a luminous globe: and the people were in drab, not a shining army on the march to meet the Future. It looked like a paragraph in a newspaper, upon which a Leading Article sits, dutifully

arousing the fat worm of sarcastic humour under the ribs of
cradled citizens, with an exposure of its excellent folly. He would
not have it laughed at; still he could not admit it as more than a
skirt of the robe of his Idea. For let none think him a mere City
merchant, millionnaire, boonfellow, or music-loving man of the
world. He had ideas to shoot across future Ages;—provide against
the shrinkage of our Coal-beds; against, and for, if you like, the
thickening, jumbling, threatening excess of population in these
Islands, in Europe, America, all over our habitable sphere.
(XLI, 493)

Victor continues with his thoughts, speculating that the death of
Mrs Burman will release him to put the Idea into practice:

Now that Mrs Burman, on her way to bliss, was no longer the
dungeon-cell for the man he would show himself to be, this name
for successes, corporate nucleus of the enjoyments, this Victor
Montgomery Radnor, intended impressing himself upon the
world as a factory of ideas. Colney's insolent charge, that the
English have no imagination—a doomed race, if it be true!—
would be confuted. For our English require but the lighted
leadership to come into cohesion, and step ranked, and chant
harmoniously the song of their benevolent aim. And that astral
head giving, as a commencement, example of the right use of
riches, the nation is one, part of the riddle of the future solved.
(XLI, 493)

The Idea then recedes as Victor contemplates the 'scheme of
Lakelands, now ruined by his incomprehensible Nesta'. This
passage is suggestive of Victor's inability to reach the Idea not
because he is passively bound to society by the connection with
Mrs Burman, but because he actively pursues material power.
Victor alludes to Nataly's lack of enthusiasm for his schemes. The
monologue suggests that he is close to awareness of his shortcomings
but he pushes this thought aside.

'After all, for a man like me, battling incessantly, a kind of
Vesuvius, I must have—can't be starved, must be fed—though,
pah! But I'm not to be questioned like other men. —But how
about an aristocracy of the contempt of distinctions? —But there
is no escaping distinctions! my aristocracy despises indulgence. —

And indulges? —Say, an exceptional nature! —Supposing a
certain beloved woman to pronounce on the case? —She cannot:
no woman can be a just judge of it.' (XLI, 494–5)

These thoughts mark the culmination of Victor's struggle to bring
the Idea into consciousness. Later in the same day the Idea returns
to him, 'full statured and embraceable'.

The death of Nataly occurs as Victor is about to make his bid for
entry into Parliament. It is ironic and tragic that it is not the death
of Mrs Burman but that of Nataly and the simultaneous ending of
Victor's public career which enables him, in madness, to reach the
Idea. Having lost both the reasons for and the capacity to take
action, Victor can express the Idea to Dudley, who recollects in
anguish some of the things he had shouted.

A notion came into the poor man, that he was the dead one of the
two, and he cried out: 'Cremation? No, Colney's right, it robs us
of our last laugh. I lie as I fall.' He 'had a confession for his Nataly,
for her only, for no one else.' He had 'an Idea.' His begging of
Dudley to listen without any punctilio (putting a vulgar oath
before it), was the sole piece of unreasonableness in the explanation of the idea: and that was not much wilder than the stuff
Dudley had read from reports of Radical speeches. (XLII, 510)

Once again the Idea comes after a fall. Whereas the first fall was
symbolic of the inherent contradiction in Victor's pursuit of both
material power and nature, the second fall results from a tragic
demonstration of the contradiction, which destroys both Nataly and
Victor.

Nesta survives to win the battle her parents fought against
society. Like Janet in *Harry Richmond*, she expresses no interest in the
estate, which stands for material possession. She puts her father's
faith in the country 'heading the world of a new epoch abjuring
materialism' (XLI, 504) into action. She and Dartrey Fenellan can
afford the courage to challenge 'that puzzled old world' which
defeated Nataly and Victor.

It is because of Nesta that Colney, in the closing words of the
book, although describing Victor as 'exposing the shallowness of the
abstract optimist', gives credit for his convictions: 'the mother and
father had kept faith with Nature'.

The attention of contemporary reviewers and critics was preoccupied with the difficulties of Meredith's syntax and in consequence their estimate of its success depended largely on more or less superficial reactions to the author's style.

Contemporary reviews received the book with less appreciation than any of Meredith's previous novels. In their range of assessment they can be divided into three groups: one shows a favourable but superficial reading of the book; another seeks a compromising critical view; a third group flatly condemns the book (see Appendix III).

More recent criticism has not found the novel's style so serious an obstacle and has consequently been able to get below the surface. This deeper penetration of the novel's structure, undoubted advance though it is, has not extended to the complexities of Meredith's characterisation. Lindsay, for example, places his emphasis on the political background of the book. He judges its theme and character in the light of the tragic consequence: 'The theme of the book is the breakdown of the great and audacious financier, Victor—his very name is emblematic; he is One of Our Conquerors—one of the new ruling-class, the bourgeoisie in their imperialist phase.' Lindsay remarks that Victor's story 'is made to represent the whole situation of his class . . . . He is drawn carefully as a man who seems the exact embodiment of a class-ideal.' Lindsay sees Victor as belonging to 'the breed of Cecil Rhodes and Joseph Chamberlain—and of Hitler'.[14]

Lindsay then, views Victor as a capitalist whose fate is deserved. In his condemnatory portrait of Victor he draws mainly on the first chapter of the book, relating the initial picture of Victor to the end of the book, and failing to take into account that the first chapter is the background out of which Victor's conflict emerges, and that the picture of Victor as entrepreneur is not given the central focus. It is rather Victor's conflict which is central, his connection with commercial power being only one aspect of the conflict.

Lindsay's view implies that Meredith's attitude to Victor was condemnatory. His own presentation becomes confused on this issue when he suggests that Hyndman served as a model for Victor, in the same way that Maxse served as a model for Beauchamp. Lindsay follows the views of Marx and Engels in regarding Hyndman as a reactionary, while claiming that Meredith regarded him as a socialist leader: 'there could have been no one worse for educating Meredith in what socialism meant, or for helping him to see the alternative to imperialist war.'[15]

Both of these assumptions are unsupported by external evidence from Meredith's or Hyndman's writings that reveal any serious commitment on Meredith's part to Hyndman's political views. Throughout their fifty-year-long friendship, Meredith rarely refers to Hyndman's socialism. In a passing remark, when he writes to Sir Francis Burnand (10 February 1908) about his memories, he says: 'And there is Hyndman, wielding the Socialist baton, to ravishing discords!' (III, 1627). On one occasion, Meredith expresses his appreciation of Hyndman's article in *Justice* which condemns the Boer War, (III, 1338) and on another he is critical of 'Hyndman's attack on the English in India' which he thought might do mischief by its lack of moderation. '*Energumene* by nature he will end with his first idea, and it is a wonder that he has not appeared waving a torch in the streets. With all this he is a good fellow' Meredith writes to John Morley in September 1906. (III, 1569) The complexity of Victor's character does not encourage the search for a model.[16]

Further in his discussion, Lindsay relates the origin of *One of Our Conquerors* to the financial crisis of 1890, remarking that 'Hyndman's comment helps us to understand Victor Radnor's anti-Semitic fears'.[17] This remark distorts the reference to Jews in *One of Our Conquerors*. Victor expresses fear of foreign capital in general, including that of Jews, rather than any specifically anti-Semitic sentiments.

Similarly, Hyndman's references to Jews in his writings concern capitalism and imperialism rather than anti-Semitism. He stands against Jewish capitalists as well as against 'the great landlords and Christian capitalists'.[18] Indeed when he deals with the crisis of 1882, it is the Union Générale, established to crush Jewish capital, that he blames for its share in bringing about the six-year long depression in Britain and Europe; he sees the basis of its establishment to be Catholic fanaticism and financial opportunism.

It is known that Meredith held 'no sympathy with the anti-Semitic opinion',[19] and it would surely therefore be unlikely that he would continue his friendship with Hyndman if he considered him to hold anti-Semitic views.

Norman Kelvin's criticism contrasts with that of Lindsay. He sees that 'Victor's Idea, whatever it is, is concerned with the welfare of humanity, or at least of England, and not with his own; not, that is, with a solution of his pressing and disturbing personal problems'. He remarks that Victor is concerned with 'good citizenship' which 'must ever remain the general ideal of conduct'. Victor's tragedy, he thinks, is inevitable because he is not able practically to conform to the current social code of morality.[20]

Where Lindsay emphasises defects in his approach to Victor's character, Kelvin over-emphasises the positive side: both critics reduce Victor to a theme. Meredith presents Victor neither with condemnation as Lindsay argues nor with compassion as Kelvin believes, but without judgement. Meredith sought to probe deeply into Victor's life and to embody theme in character. In *One of Our Conquerors* he succeeds in presenting the theme of the book through the experience of the character.

It is perhaps a measure of Meredith's own satisfaction with his achievement in these areas that he was led, unusually, to express some enthusiasm about the book several years after its appearance. He writes to J. H. Hutchinson: 'You mention *One of Our Conquerors* with revulsion. It is a trying piece of work. I had to look at it recently, and remembered my annoyance in correcting proofs. But, strange to say, it held me.' (III, 1573) He then continues to draw attention to the emphasis he made on character rather than theme.

Oscar Wilde's comment on Meredith's characters applies particularly, I think, to *One of Our Conquerors*. 'His people not merely live, but they live in thought. One can see them from myriad points of view. They are suggestive. There is soul in them and around them. . . . And he who made them . . . has never allowed the public to dictate to him . . . , but has gone on intensifying his own personality and producing his own individual work.'[21]

6 *The Amazing Marriage*: the Marriage of Contraries

In a letter to R. L. Stevenson (16 April 1879) Meredith wrote:

> My Egoist has been out of my hands for a couple of months, but Kegan Paul does not wish to publish it before October. I don't think you will like it; I doubt if those who care for my work will take to it at all. And for this reason, after doing my best with it, I am in no hurry to see it appear. It is a Comedy, with only half of me in it, unlikely, therefore, to take either the public or my friends. . . . I am about one quarter through *The Amazing Marriage*, which I promise you, you shall like better. (II, 569)

And in another letter to G. W. Foote (30 May 1879) he wrote: 'I finished a 3 volume work [*The Egoist*] rapidly, and as it comes mainly from the head and has nothing to kindle imagination, I thirsted to be rid of it soon after conception'. (II, 573)

Meredith's reaction against a finished work and his yearning for a new one to start is not unusual, but his reaction against *The Egoist* after he had finished it was stronger than usual. As we can see from his correspondence, Meredith wasted no time in starting a new novel, though he was still ill after he had finished *The Egoist*. The main reason behind this prompt action lies obviously in Meredith's dissatisfaction with the fiction of dry reason as much as in his inclination towards the kind of fiction which is able 'to kindle imagination'. The result was *The Amazing Marriage*, the earliest draft of which was begun shortly after *The Egoist*, and though *The Egoist* brought Meredith more popularity than he perhaps anticipated, his attitude towards dry reason and lively imagination was unchanged, as he continued to work on *The Amazing Marriage* long after the publication of *The Egoist*.

Despite the various complex stages through which the novel passed, during a period of about fifteen years of intermittent work on it, *The Amazing Marriage* remains essentially a recast of *The*

Egoist, but the more Meredith reworked it the further he moved
from the spirit of the earlier novel. A close examination of the two
early incomplete drafts in the light of the printed version shows
Meredith's attempt to overcome the limitations he felt in the
presentation of Willoughby especially and the comedy of dry reason
in general.

The two drafts in question are the Cole and Nicholl drafts,
referred to hereafter as *A* and *B*. *A* is 187 leaves, *B* 165 leaves—both
written on one side.[1]

These two early drafts show Meredith working on an egoistic
character who is an individual rather than a pattern, and who is
endowed with imagination and power.

The characteristic limitation in *The Egoist* is the static nature of
action as Willoughby repeats the same pattern of behaviour towards
each woman partner he meets. Motive in him is related directly to
action. Willoughby is an unprotected child (xxxiv, 421) who
seeks protection and no sooner is he deserted by one woman than he
turns to another. He lacks individuality and development because
he is the material in which a predetermined theme is worked out.
Both narrator and antagonist collaborate to reveal what he tries to
hide. The reconciliation reached in the end marks the triumph of
the Comic Spirit rather than a genuine change in Willoughby's
character.

Like Willoughby, Fleetwood is the egoist as beast, but unlike him
he is not a tame one. 'It was the fever of rivalry entering Fleetwood,
and he had the sense of loving her like a beast of prey.' (*B*, 131)
Henrietta 'let the minutes fly, unaware that a hunter was after her'
(*B*, 251) His pursuit of Carinthia when he sees her for the first time is
described as a 'chase', 'well hunt, a wild falcon on horseback!' (*B*,
257) He says to Henrietta: 'I'm not a tame cat, I'm more of a
leopard!' (*B*, 273) After Henrietta had mentioned the name of
Chillon for the first time in front of Fleetwood, 'he felt both the
wrath of a husband at the lover's name on her mouth, and the
exultation of a lover in his power to dispossess the husband. From
presently to prospectively he was either of the characters by fits; so
little in his breathing body, that if he had caught the beautiful
creature to his breast with her consent, he would not have known a
pleasure beyond the tiger's.' (*A*, 296) Fleetwood's agressiveness
would extend to Henrietta's 'heart' (*A*, 295), or to her 'soul'.
(*B*, 265)

In his attempt to win Henrietta, Fleetwood, like Willoughby, distinguishes himself from the rest of the world by his claim to know her better: 'I say I understand you, read you: and I don't think of you as the world does,' he says to Henrietta. (B, 280) But, unlike Willoughby, he has no fear of the world to curb his action: 'Not the whole world can force me to give up my treasure'. (B, 274) Fleetwood is an aggressive egoist who would not accept any connection with Henrietta short of marriage. In a reply reminiscent of Clara's, Henrietta says to Fleetwood: 'Friends you have, Lord Fleetwood; only learn to know them.' He answers: 'Your husband's name is Russett.' (A, 279) Later in a passage which expresses his vigour and imagination he says: 'You give me a friend, you give me a mate. My life I never asked for; my wife I did. No wonder I love my wife better than my life. There's not a doubt of the two. Rietta! Fairer, dearer, twice me! Mistress of me and all I have.' (A, 282–3) Earlier in B the narrative voice records that nothing less than Henrietta's death would satisfy him in his state of frustrating mixed emotions: 'He felt the shock of that encounter [between Chillon and Henrietta], tasted the mingling of the bitter dwarf and the venomous, admired, envied, hated, yearned, abhorred, galloped through every act of the drama up to the exquisite reptile's death— nothing less. Pain seeks appeasement and the extinction of the traitress presents it. She dies! Then good night to life!' (B, 132)

A picture of contradictory traits in Fleetwood appears in detail. Meredith uses various descriptions: 'In the way of the greater number of young men, the son of wealth and title perused an imaginary self attentively during the intervals when his engine self was not at high pressure'. (A, 127) Later comes a description of the two selves in action: 'The brighter portion of him richly gilded the foul; and his confession to the existence of a darker sanctioned his belief in the transcendently fair' (A, 129) A similar description appears in B but with more details seemingly intended to clarify the interaction between the two selves:

Lord Fleetwood perused an imaginary self with attention in the intervals when his engine-self was not at full speed; and quite as much as the greater number consent to do, he corrected the imaginary with a record of some of the deeds of the engine. An agreeable semi-realistic picture resulted, which he could take to be faithful. The fairer part of him gilded the foul, and his candid admission of the existence of a fouler sanctioned his belief in the extremely fair.

The description goes on to show Fleetwood's awareness of his egoism: 'He could be devilish, he knew.' At the same time he demonstrates in terms of action that he is 'large of soul, generous, fierily a worshipper of the good, the gallant, the lofty and wise'. The narrator then intervenes to explain the nature of action and consequence of conflict.

> Deduce me, then, that if our deeds are a network of contradictions, and we with our aim at the purely virtuous, have sometimes pushed an arbitrary will and a sceptical fury past legitimate bounds to works of mischief, it is distinguishable as the fault of mankind. To swim the stream and wing the air, our imaginary self must have it so. The excessive badness of the human blood is the cause of our deviations. We sacrifice them on the altar of our higher nature sadly, but in the lump. (*B*, 129)

The significant alteration which occurs between the two drafts and the final version lies, I think, in the shift of emphasis from the story of Fleetwood and Henrietta to that of Fleetwood and Carinthia. It is likely that this was prompted by Meredith's desire to prevent the second story being overshadowed by the first. Hence Meredith's speculation over the misinterpretation of the purpose of the book, even after the alteration, when he wrote to William M. Colles (February 1893): 'Next week you shall have the opening of *The Amazing Marriage*—called by one paper *The Amazing Lover*'. (II, 1122)

The alteration can be viewed within the light of Meredith's lifelong preoccupation with motive and action and his attempt to achieve a balanced emphasis on each in the narrative. Behind the action of the System in *The Ordeal*, for example, lies the motive of Sir Austin's wrath with his wife, and the story of his motive which remains lurking in the background and only hinted at through the course of action. Motive procedes action. It was presumably Meredith's plan in *The Ordeal* to show action (and its tragic consequence) determined by motive.

The plot of *The Egoist* involves three stories: that of Willoughby and Constancia, which has been reduced to an allusion and serves only as a motive; that of Willoughby and Clara, which forms the action of the book; and that of Willoughby and Laetitia, which comes as a reconciliation. The three stories are similarly controlled by the sequence of time and the plausibility of cause and effect. The story which precedes forms the motive for that which follows.

Meredith's intention that *The Amazing Marriage* should stand in opposition to the pattern of theme and character in *The Egoist* provoked certain characteristics of presentation. One is the imaginative quality in Fleetwood's character; another is a wider range of action prompted by a detailed picture of two stories; a third characteristic is related to the nature of interaction between the two stories in that both collaborate to present different aspects of character rather than being causally interrelated.

The shift of narrative interest from the story of Fleetwood and Henrietta to that of Fleetwood and Carinthia created problems for the design which were not solved in the early drafts of the novel. One problem arose from the danger that the overwhelming effect of the picture of Fleetwood the lover would overshadow that of Fleetwood the husband. The Fleetwood of the early drafts is the most imaginative and eloquent of Meredith's characters, indeed, of Ben Jonson's comic protagonists such as Volpone. Any drastic change in Fleetwood's character such as becoming a husband to anyone other than Henrietta would reduce him in stature and perhaps make him unconvincing.

Another problem arises from the slowness of action in the wooing scene itself. The scene here presents the realised situation of Fleetwood's insistence and Henrietta's resistence which parallels in its nature of limitation that of Willoughby and Clara. Another limitation which has a parallel in *The Egoist* is the time sequence of love and marriage, but marriage as reconciliation would have less credibility for Fleetwood than Willoughby. It is perhaps for this reason that marriage in the final version happens at a much earlier stage than in the early drafts. The action of the novel as printed wastes no time in introducing Carinthia and the amazing marriage. This obviously led to the reduction of the long wooing scene at Baden which occupies the main part of the two drafts. The result is that the picture of Fleetwood the lover gives way to that of Fleetwood the husband, but without suppressing its dominant effect since Fleetwood's infatuation with Henrietta continues to emerge in the course of action along with Fleetwood's involvement with Carinthia.

However the main reason behind the abandonment of the early plan lies, I think, in Meredith's intention to intensify the contrast between *The Egoist* and *The Amazing Marriage* since the picture of Fleetwood, the imaginative egoist of the drafts, appeared on its own to be inadequate for a deep contrast over the several years of intermittent work on the book. Though Fleetwood's character in the final version loses the lyrical intensity of the early picture, it gains in complexity. The main points of Meredith's achievement in *The Amazing Marriage* are: the complexity of Fleetwood's character; the independence of Woodseer as a minor character; and the development of Carinthia as a female character. The concept of nature is explored in each of these characters. A critical consideration of these points will bring us close to the purpose of Meredith's final complete achievement in fiction.

The complexity of Fleetwood's character consists essentially in the mixture of egoism and nature that his character contains. He lives with these contraries, and this creates in him a continually shifting conflict. It is his link with nature that gives Fleetwood imagination and power, and his love of natural beauty (the external aspect of the concept of nature) provides the objectification of this feeling, just as Willoughby's scientific pursuits objectify his domination by 'dry reason'. The concept of nature in *The Egoist* is not as integrated a part of the structure of character as it becomes in *The Amazing Marriage*. Nature is introduced as a kind of *deus ex machina*: it comes to Willoughby only to demonstrate the power of the comic spirit. Clara is granted nature only to become herself an egoist, as the conflict between them continues to be between one who insists and the other who resists. Christopher Caudwell comments perceptively when he says that 'Both want their own ways, and only one can get it'.[2] Vernon Whitford too is a cold and rational character, and nature as a power in character and action remains unexplored in *The Egoist*.

While Willoughby's relationships with women are motivated only by the egoistic desire for protection, Fleetwood is attracted to his women partners by a realisation of their intrinsic and individual qualities as well as by his needs for egoistic self-gratification. His admiration of Henrietta's beauty, his proposal to Carinthia, and later on his effort to become reconciled with her, are acts of nature.

Fleetwood is aware of the conflicts within him: 'Now, if the fact were declared and attested, if her [Henrietta's] shallowness were seen proved, one might get free of the devil she plants in the breast. Absolutely to despise her would be release, and it would allow of his tasting Carinthia's charm, reluctantly acknowledged; not "money of the country" beside that golden Henrietta's.' (XXI, 221) He is however unable to take action to resolve conflict, and even when he becomes detached enough to recognise egoism in himself and nature in Carinthia, he cannot completely free himself from egoism for he continues to scheme for vengeance upon Chillon. He is aware of his lack of will to sever past from present when he says to Woodseer: 'Did you ever tell anyone, that there's not an act of a man's life lies dead behind him, but it is blessing or cursing him every step he takes?' (XL, 420)

Fleetwood's recognition of nature (as expressed in the emergence of the disillusioned self) in connection with his asserted love for Carinthia towards the end of the book can be viewed in the light of Proustian 'time regained'. His vision of partnership with Carinthia first emerges during his walk through the foreign pine forest, from Woodseer's description. It is then realised when he meets her. In this first stage, Fleetwood's vision is not established but vaguely captured, and lacks 'faith'. It is lost after the proposal, which is similar in nature to Sir Austin's 'System', in the sense that each is partly motivated by nature (Sir Austin's love for his son and Fleetwood's love for Carinthia) and partly by egoism. Fleetwood's vision is achieved, in its second stage, when it acquires faith as he identifies Carinthia as the person with whom his partnership in quest can be established. This is displayed in his outburst to Carinthia: 'I have learnt—learnt what I am, what you are; I have to climb a height to win back the wife I threw away. She was unknown to me; I to myself nearly as much.' (XLIV, 462) The narrative voice records his restored passion 'for a woman he had dreamed of in his younger time, doubting that he would ever meet the fleshly woman to impose it'.(XLVI, 493)

Woodseer, the observer in the book, is given more prominence than any of Meredith's previous commentators. He is not simply a *persona* like the Philosopher in *Emilia in England*. Nor is he a one-sided character controlled by the authorial voice to serve as a thematic background for the protagonist like Dr Shrapnel in *Beauchamp's Career*. Though he studies and observes nature, he does not represent its essence for he violates it on some occasions, such as when he submits to Livia's seductiveness and when he indulges in gambling. He differs from Fleetwood in that he is able after such lapses to restore his harmony with nature.

Woodseer, without losing his individuality as a character, acts as a catalyst in the interplay of nature between Fleetwood and Carinthia. He sees through the character of Fleetwood: 'You hang for the Fates to settle which is to be smothered in you, the man or the lord—and it ends in the monk, if you hang much longer.' (XXXI,

328) On another occasion the narrative voice records Woodseer's observation which, by implication, expresses Fleetwood's conflict: 'Men hating Nature are insane. Women and Nature are close. If it is rather general to hate Nature and maltreat women, we begin to see why the world is a mad world.' (xxxv, 363)

It is through Woodseer's record of his impression of Carinthia that Fleetwood first knows of her.

If Fleetwood lives in the world of his own contradictions, Carinthia is caught in such a world but one which is not wholly of her own making; and the interaction between nature in her and society outside is what gradually shapes her character.

In the early part of the book—from Carinthia's departure from the mountains to her settling in England at Admiral Fakenham's house—she can be seen as a figure in romance where she grows in and with nature. In the middle part—from her marriage until her settling in Whitechapel—she is seen emerging from romance to a state of disillusion. It is not until later in the book that the reader distinctly grasps her character and realises how the earlier parts are integrated in the later one.

Early in the book, romance, in terms of which Carinthia envisages life, is reality. The different stages of her life are marked by the changes in her states of feeling. Her character develops in response to the changing circumstances of her life, and the change is reflected in varying ways in which her character is presented.

The nature of development in Carinthia's character demonstrates Meredith's conception of romance as being a certain level of consciousness which is associated with innocence. It is one stage of reality where a simple but disturbed vision is dominant. With experience comes disillusion, developing the character's consciousness of reality. Realism here implies a change of sensibility and a narrowing of the distance between the reader and character.

In the sequence of events, marriage and the birth of her child are the major incidents which bring about change in Carinthia's character and transition from one stage of awareness to another. The baby picture is an objectification of her feelings in the later stage as natural beauty does earlier. While she was unable to perceive egoism in Fleetwood's vengeful attitude towards her brother, she realises his egoism through his lack of interest in the child for she sees herself in the child.

Marriage on Carinthia's part has the spontaneity of nature; it is an expression of her need for love: as she says to her brother, she 'cannot exist without being loved'. (v, 46) Marriage is, however, also an act of conformity with society. When Carinthia expresses her awareness that she is a burden on her brother, he suggests that she marry and become 'a blessing to a husband'. (v, 47)

Meredith exploits the marriage convention to expose the social background against which Carinthia's character develops. The marriage shows that one partner exploits the other, and shows society and egoism in action against nature. For Meredith's women, marriage is the only way to establish partnership with men in society. Before Carinthia, Browny of *Lord Ormont and His Aminta*, and Diana of *Diana of the Crossways* are driven to their first marriage by the social pressure brought to bear on them because of their living alone.

Once marriage (or engagement in Clara's case) takes place, female characters begin to realise the crudity of the act. Their reaction against society expresses itself in the form of their quest for love, driven this time by the negative power of egoism as demonstrated in the emptiness of the loveless union. In Clara, Diana and Browny the quest ends triumphantly with their disentanglement from their partners to establish a new union based on love and respect.

Carinthia's reaction goes further than disentanglement from the egoism of Fleetwood. Through her, Meredith explores the question of the emancipation of women further and with more gradual development in character than ever before. Carinthia's change of sensibility comes through suffering during which she develops from naïveté to disillusionment. When Clara, for example, becomes disillusioned about Willoughby's proposal she has not actually suffered from him, and her antagonism to him is basically motivated by her desire to avoid suffering. Suffering in Diana and Browny as a result of the loveless union is presented without any considerable detail. In Nataly, Meredith presents a picture of suffering so deep that any emergence of reconciliation might seem unconvincing. It is not unlikely that the positive element in Carinthia was partly motivated by the critical reaction of the reviews to the passivity in Nataly. Carinthia puts in practice what Nataly experiences in silence, or what is expressed in *One of Our Conquerors* by minor characters like Mademoiselle Louise de Seilles, Mrs Marsett and Nesta.

Carinthia emerges from her confrontation with Fleetwood as the new woman. She is the kind of social rebel of the time who is depicted in works like Grant Allen's *The Woman Who Did* (which came out at about the same time as *The Amazing Marriage*). But the rebellious Miss Barton is presented by means of melodrama and sentimentality.[3]

Carinthia is the English Nora and the relevant aspects of *The Amazing Marriage* bear much resemblance to the plot of *A Doll's House*.[4] Interestingly enough, the play appeared in the same year that *The Egoist* was published, and when Meredith began to work on *The Amazing Marriage*, Ibsen and his play continued to arouse special interest in this country during the following years.[5]

Carinthia and Nora embark on marriage with the womanly ideal of self-sacrifice as a heroic aim. Like Nora, Carinthia awakes to the idea that marriage should not bring degradation and that duty to a husband is not the most sacred duty. There emerges the desire to exercise the right of a woman to her individuality. Carinthia's reply to Fleetwood that she will guard her rooms if he breaks in recalls Nora's slamming the door in Helmer's face.[6] The confrontation between Nora and Helmer is very reminiscent of the scene 'Between Carinthia and Her Lord' of Chapter XXXVII.

The Amazing Marriage goes beyond Carinthia's rejection. After Carinthia demonstrates her capacity to live in society without marriage, becoming instead devoted to her child, friends and public life, she accepts Owain Wythan in marriage. Carinthia's act is not, as Barbara Hardy takes it, anticlimactic to her revolutionary attitude.[7] It suggests that she rejects marriage as an institution and to an egoist husband, but not marriage in itself.

Carinthia wins the battle which is forced (by the Comic Spirit) on Laetitia to win. Had she won it in the same way as Laetitia, that is, by accepting Fleetwood's offer of reconciliation and dictating her own terms, the consequence would have been another drift to the triumph of egoism and Carinthia would eventually have become, like Laetitia, an egoist. Meredith does not imply that the conflict between husband and wife essentially involves hostility between the two sexes and that men are egoists and women are not. His tendency to present men as egoists is determined by the fact that it is men who are given power in society. This is demonstrated earlier in *One of Our Conquerors* by the dialogue between Louise de Seilles and Nesta when the first says: 'Oh, there are bad women as well as bad men: but men have the power and the lead, and they take advantage of it; and then they turn round and execrate us for not having what they have robbed us of!' (XXVIII, 341)[8]

For a critical view of Carinthia's character it is important to consider the totality of her vision as she progresses from the state of illusion to that of disillusion; and by ignoring the nature of development in Carinthia current reviews and later criticism fall short of an adequate appreciation of her portrait. *The Bookman*, for example, considers 'the Carinthia that plays an active part is a bore'.[9] *The Echo* fails to appreciate the nature of development in character. The review remarks that Carinthia, like Fleetwood, is 'guilty of the most extravagant self-contradiction', and that she 'exhibits inconsistencies which are even harder to reconcile'.[10] *The Pall Mall Gazette* sees Carinthia's change of sensibility to be unreal, commenting that the scene of the proposal 'remains throughout the whole story unconvincing and unreal, a canopy of doubtfulness from which the heroine never quite succeeds in emerging'.[11] *The Globe* denies Carinthia the intellect of Diana or the charm of Clara.[12]

M. Sturge Henderson considers Carinthia's rejection of reconciliation with Fleetwood unethical and describes her attitude as 'strangely unimaginative'.[13] Later on Norman Kelvin adopts and elaborates the same view: 'It is, strangely, her indifference to happiness—her lack of a real imaginative grasp of it—so that she is quite unaware of risk and possible sacrifice.'[14]

The main flaw in such criticism lies in its overlooking the nature of contraries around which the life of character revolves (see Appendix IV). Fleetwood has both egoism and nature in him, illusion and disillusion. The complexity of his character is revealed through the action, for which Meredith offers no explanation. Nor does Meredith explain the emergence of Carinthia's character from a state of inexperience and simplicity to a state of experience and complexity. His lifelong preoccupation with the point of view and his tendency to stand back from his characters are demonstrated in the book through the narrators and a detailed discussion of their role can help us towards a fuller appreciation of this purpose.

Meredith's solution to the problem of the role of the narrator and the point of view was often to introduce a subsidiary narrator to collaborate in the presentation of the narrative. In *Emilia in England*, for example, he introduces the Philosopher; in *Harry Richmond* he alludes to 'Dame Fortune'; and in *One of Our Conquerors* to 'Dame Nature'. But in none of these attempts does the subsidiary narrator acquire any considerable presence in the narrative, and the question of the point of view is solved by devices such as the first

person narrator in *Harry Richmond* and the stream of consciousness in
One of Our Conquerors.[15]

Narration in *The Amazing Marriage* is presented as a joint effort
shared by the novelist–narrator (referred to henceforward as the
narrator) and Dame Gossip. They stand respectively for the two
extreme points of reference in the criticism of the time. Dame Gossip
stands for story-telling and romance,[16] the narrator for character
analysis.

Dame Gossip, we know, is in possession of the documents of the
story. She undertakes the responsibility of telling the history of the
Buccaneers in the first four chapters of the book and later she tells
the story of the twenty Welsh cavaliers. (xxxiv) Beside the story-
telling as a mode of narration, dialogue is occasionally used to
present the events, as in Chapter xxviii. This satisfies for Meredith
the issue of when to narrate and when to dramatise.

But the presence of Dame Gossip is not solely technical. The
confrontation between her and the narrator raises the serious issue
of realism such as is presented in an interpolated passage which
describes the Dame's effort to create a make-believe world: 'Dame
Gossip boils. Her one idea of animation is to have her *dramatis
personae* in violent motion, always the biggest foremost; and, indeed,
that is the way to make them credible, for the wind they raise and
the succession of collisions.' (xx, 209) The narrator here points to
the lack of human vitality in characters which are revealed through
sensational incident, remarking on 'her endless ejaculations over the
mystery of Life, the inscrutability of character,—in a plain world, in
the midst of such readable people!' The interpolation concludes
with a comment which though overtly concerned with the Dame
obliquely refers to writers of romance with their concentration on
violent emotions: 'To preserve Romance (we exchange a sky for a
ceiling if we let it go), we must be inside the heads of our people as
well as the hearts, more than shaking the kaleidoscope of hurried
spectacles, in days of a growing activity of the head.' This sentence
reiterates the plan Meredith described to Stevenson to write a new
'Egoist' characterised by the balance between head and heart.

Later in the book the narrator points out the limitations of story-
telling (romance as taken by the Dame) when he describes the
Dame's 'parrot cry of "John Rose Mackrell!" with her head's loose
shake over the smack of her lap, to convey the contemporaneous
tipsy relish of the rich good things he said on the subject of the
contest, indicates the kind of intervention it would be'. The narrator

intervenes 'to save the story from having its vein tied.' (xxvi, 263) A similar example of the competition between the Dame and the narrator occurs in the early draft in a transitional passage which links Fleetwood's jealous wrath with Henrietta to his anxiety on seeing Carinthia for the first time: 'And now you know what he has on board in the way of steam-generating machinery, as you should know of the leader of a story, unless you are all for Dame Gossip's gaps-mouth miraculous; and now, as they say of freighted vessels, the rest is between sea and sky; we are out of haven.' (B, 255) Meredith alluded to the tension between the two narrators in a letter to R. L. Stevenson while he was writing the book: 'Dame Gossip pulls one way and I another'. (iii, 1153)

However the narrator, in his turn, succumbs to the Dame when the occasion arises: 'She would be off with us on one of her whirling cyclones or elemental mad waltzes, if a step were taken to the lecturing-desk. We are so far in her hands that we have to keep her quiet.' The narrative voice here indicates a major limitation in the narrator's method. It implies an attack on contemporary realism for its excessive concern with the 'scrutability' of character. Dame Gossip refuses to be controlled by the narrator or even to listen to him: 'She will not hear of the reasons and the change of reasons for one thing and the other. Things were so: narrate them, and let readers do their reflections for themselves, she says, denouncing our conscientious as the direct road downward to the dreadful modern appeal to the senses and assault on them for testimony to the veracity of everything described.' (xxxv, 367) This is an indirect appeal to reviewers and critics to accept the inscrutability of character when the Dame narrates, as well as a warning against expecting the 'scrutability' of contemporary realism, which they would find lacking in the Dame's narration.

However, reviewers and critics overlook the nature of joint narrative in the book, and the unified purpose lying behind the structure of contraries. In their criticism they do not acknowledge the delicate balance Meredith establishes between the two narrators and that the narrative structure reflects on the life of character as presented in the book. It is important, I think, to notice that Meredith did not intend to reconcile the contraries in the picture of Fleetwood and Carinthia. Fleetwood has in him the social egoist and the natural man—both exist side by side and sometimes act upon him simultaneously. He is capable of using and abusing imagination. Carinthia emerges from irrational to rational nature.

In her last confrontation with Fleetwood there is conflict in her between social duty and natural inclination. Some of her acts, such as protecting Fleetwood from a mad dog, imply a combination of nobility and savagery. Nature in the book is both sensuous and spiritual and the contrast is demonstrated in the movement from the literal to the figurative as seen in the association of Carinthia with mountains and plains. These contraries are partly narrated and partly analysed, but in no case are 'the reasons and the change of reasons for one thing and the other' given.

The intricate design in *The Amazing Marriage* seems to have helped Meredith to stand back from characters and to abstain from passing judgement on their actions. It was with this intention that Meredith embarked on *The Amazing Marriage* immediately after he finished *The Egoist*. But as he went on writing 'an egoist' which does not come 'mainly from the head' and has enough 'to kindle imagination' he realised that dry reason was still making its appearance in the form of the narrative comment. In the earlier drafts which Meredith abandoned before completion the narrator often steps aside to give reasons for Fleetwood's egoistic behaviour especially to explain his proposal to Carinthia and to relate his ill-treatment of her directly to Henrietta's rejection of him. Fleetwood's jealousy is not suppressed altogether from the printed novel, but it is not emphasised as a source of motivation. At the end of the book there is a passage which retrospectively shows that Fleetwood's proposal to Carinthia was an act of nature:

> He believed—some have said his belief was not in error—that the woman to aid and make him man and be the star in human form to him, was miraculously revealed on the day of his walk through the foreign pine forest, and his proposal to her at the ducal ball was an inspiration of his Good Genius, continuing to his marriage morn, and then running downwards, like an overstrained reel, under the leadership of his Bad. (XLVII, 508)

When Meredith wrote to Stevenson that he was one quarter through *The Amazing Marriage* he was evidently accommodating the other half of him (of imagination) left out in *The Egoist*. The excessive power of imagination in Fleetwood seemed to have invited the rational mind of the narrator to explain the nature of egoism. Meredith probably realised then that though he was presenting a different picture of egoism his point of view was not very different in that egoism both in Willoughly and Fleetwood was a source of condemnation. With the lapse of approximately fifteen years between the early draft and the last complete version of the book, Meredith seems to have developed control over the narrative voice and to have passed the rational side to the character itself. As a result *The Amazing Marriage* succeeds in giving a more rounded embodiment of its author's vision than had appeared in his previous fiction.

It is regrettable that Stevenson died just one month before the first instalment of the book appeared in *The Scriber's Magazine*, and did not live to see how *The Amazing Marriage* eventually came to synthesise the two halves of his friend's vision.

7 Conclusion

The complexity of the development of Meredith's fiction has not been fully explored by critics. This can be well demonstrated from the critical consideration of Meredith's later works which appeared in the 1890s; for though *One of Our Conquerors* and *The Amazing Marriage* mark a considerable change in Meredith's fiction, critics of the period either referred only casually to them or ignored their merits completely. Le Gallienne, for example, saw Meredith as the writer of *The Ordeal of Richard Feverel*: 'Of Mr. Meredith's work published since 1890 one may say generally that it is remarkably of a piece with the work that preceded it. Its excellences and its faults are the same, and its creative youth is as lusty and prodigal as that which created *Richard Feverel*.'[1] In her study of Meredith's novels, which along with Le Gallienne's, form the first two extensive studies on Meredith, Hannah Lynch does not even mention *One of Our Conquerors*, though it was available, if only in serial.

One may argue that behind the silence over Meredith's later works lies the fact of Meredith's sustained interest in the novel as a genre at a time when the tendency in the arts and literature was towards shorter genres. Conder painted small objects; Dawson wrote short stories; and the one-act play, already popular on the continent, was beginning to acquire popularity in England. Poetry and the essay flourished more than ever before. Emphasis in this period was on form and style and contemporary references to Meredith's writing frequently reflect this bias which can be illustrated from the few critical allusions to Meredith in *The Yellow Book*.

Morton Fullerton, for example, expressed his admiration for Meredith in a sonnet.[2] G. S. Street saw Meredith as a writer of short stories. He seems to have come across the collection of the short stories published in book form and wrongly supposed that the collection was his last published work.[3] Street criticises Meredith's prose for lack of ease and rhythm and for being unnecessarily hard to understand.[4]

In a later issue of *The Yellow Book* a similar reaction against Meredith's fiction was evident. John M. Robertson remarked that with the exception of Zola's *La Terre* he found *One of Our Conquerors* the most difficult novel he had ever read, and though he first thought that *Lord Ormont and His Aminta* was easy enough, he decided after a few chapters to stop reading Meredith altogether.[5] W. G. Blakie Murdock criticises Meredith for the same thing. He remarks that Meredith's dialogue is written 'more often in Meredithese than in the vernacular'. He, however, gives Meredith credit for his interest in the young men and their heroic campaign.[6]

Sympathetic views of Meredith are not different in nature, for they lack any specific reference to Meredith's works and their allusions are to style and form, as the literary canons of the period required. For example, Arthur Symons, the editor of *The Savoy* sees Meredith as a 'Decadent', by which he means one who exhibits 'that learned corruption of language by which style ceases to be organic and becomes, in the pursuit of some new expressiveness or beauty, deliberately abnormal'. He comments that 'Meredith's style is as self-conscious as Mallarmé's. But, unlike many self-conscious styles, it is alive in every fibre.' He appreciates Meredith's decadence as a novelist and prefers him to any other novelist despite his breaking of the conventions of the novel.[7]

Bernard Muddiman, a critic of the period, found it difficult to decide where to locate Meredith in the movement, for he could neither put him with the conventional Henley-Pan of the *National Observer* such as Stevenson and Kipling nor with the unconventional young men of the nineties. In his discussion of the novel he takes George Moore as an example. But he comments: 'It must be at once admitted, one fails to recall a great novel. It is true that the great Victorians, Meredith and Hardy, were hard at work in their time; but, then, neither of these writers belongs to this movement.'[8]

It is true that the novel as a genre was overshadowed by the shorter genres which emerged and became popular towards the end of the century; but this should not lead to the conclusion that the older, longer genre was incapable of accommodating the spirit of the time, nor should it imply that a novelist like Meredith was unaware of this spirit and unable to give it expression. Muddiman would perhaps have recognised in Meredith the 'staying power' which was lacking in young writers had he not been overwhelmed by the novelty of the movement of younger writers. Or if the novel appealed to Muddiman, and other critics of the period, he would have been able to trace in Meredith's later works various aspects of the movement itself.

One of Our Conquerors, for example, has much of the '*fin de Siecle*' mood in it.[9] Victor's life is, in a sense, a sustained protest such as that of Wilde, Symons, Johnson, Davidson, Beerbohm and others. His uncertainty, indecisiveness, restlessness and morbidity, are all characteristic traits of the life the young artists lived and tended to express in their art. Like them Victor finds in art a refuge from his dilemma. He, too, yearns for a 'new era' and is at odds with the conventions of society. The complex division in Victor is a demonstration of a typical current preoccupation with the divided self: a preoccupation also exemplified in *The Picture of Dorian Gray* by Lord Henry's questioning of the rationality of man.[10]

Other aspects of the movement can be traced in *The Amazing Marriage* as well. There is, for example, Fleetwood's life of contraries; and it is perhaps Meredith's awareness of the growing complexity of life towards the end of the century which prompted him to abandon the simple portrayal of Fleetwood found in the two earlier drafts. Woodseer's occasional indulgence in Bohemian life is typical. More typical still is the quest for freedom as expressed in the person of Carinthia. However *The Amazing Marriage* remains less representative of the movement than *One of Our Conquerors*, a close examination of which shows that it is one of the most representative novels of the art and life of the period together.

Meredith, then, while maintaining his confidence in the older genre, worked out his own way of conveying the new spirit but without succeeding in changing old enemies (represented by contemporary reviewers) or in winning friends in the new organs of the movement.

One regrets that silence over Meredith's later work lasted well into this century. In the course of his study Robert Sitwell makes hasty, irrelevant, and superficial remarks on *One of Our Conquerors* and ignores *The Amazing Marriage*, while he thinks that *The Ordeal* and *The Egoist* are the greatest of Meredith's works.[11]

In more recent studies Meredith's later works have not been given, comparatively speaking, enough attention, for critics continued hostile to them on the assumption of the growing difficulty of style in Meredith.[12] Sassoon, for example, considers that Meredith's style was becoming more difficult towards the end of his writing career. With such an attitude (which is typical) Sassoon ignores the fact that the last three novels vary greatly among themselves in style though written within the same short span of time. *One of Our Conquerors* was followed by a much simpler novel, *Lord Ormont and His Aminta*. *The Amazing Marriage* was not as simple as the previous novel but it is certainly simpler than *One of Our Conquerors*. This phenomenon, however, has been noticed by some modern critics, not without puzzlement. Lindsay, for example, considers *Lord Ormont and His Aminta* 'a slight work, as though Meredith is taking a breath between the hectic fury of *One of Our Conquerors* and the lyrical intensity of his last novel'.[13] In her essay on *Lord Ormont and His Aminta* and *The Amazing Marriage* Barbara Hardy notices 'the sharp difference in fictional quality between the two works' despite 'their chronological neighbourhood and their strong affinity of story and theme'.[14]

But difficulty in Meredith is not a question of chronological development nor is it a matter of coincidence as Lindsay and Barbara Hardy tend to think. It was determined partly by the degree of concession Meredith was prepared to make when writing a new book, and when its predecessor had met with a hostile reception. Concerning *One of Our Conquerors* Meredith wrote to Clement K. Shorter: 'Andrew Lang gives me criticism, and I take it in good part . . . I have at present a feeling of the Fates in conspiracy with a frowning country to forbid further action of my pen. And, by the way, as to the publishers, if the run against this novel should put my present men out of pocket, I shall feel bound to give them a chance of indemnification with the offer of a more generally readable.'[15] Though Meredith in another letter (June 1891) wrote that there would be no further chance of peace between him and the reviewers, he later designed *Lord Ormont and His Aminta* to affect a reconciliation with reviewers and publishers alike. When Meredith was less conscious of or concerned with reviewers he felt less restricted in presenting the full intensity of his vision and, as a result, the freer rein on his artistic bent led to greater obscurity.

However the main source of difficulty is related to Meredith's increasing desire to widen the scope of his characterisation, and in this study I hope I have shown how Meredith developed from one novel to another rather than from one period of writing to another; for Meredith is not like James whose later work can be distinguished from his earlier quite simply on grounds of difficulty. At the same time I hope this study has demonstrated that development in Meredith's fiction is a matter of perpetual renewal of theme and character presentation. To say with Pritchett that Meredith's novels are all stories of education leads us nowhere because the story of education is carried out by each character in a different way. Richard Feverel is, for example, as much distinguished from Harry Richmond as Werther from Wilhelm Meister. It similarly does not help us towards any understanding of Meredith's fiction to be told by Christopher Caudwell that all Meredith's characters are careerists, for each character presented has a different purpose, and the energy each has for living out this purpose varies from one character to another. Richard, for example, embarks on life eventually to come to terms with it; Beauchamp to change it; Victor to solve its conflict; Fleetwood to live its contraries. The common ground against which characters move in the novels forms only a façade which, if emphasised, leads to a misinterpretation or underestimating of purpose.

Generalisation on Meredith's fiction still prevails. A modern reviewer, echoing the criticism of *The Spectator*, has claimed that Meredith sowed the seed of his unpopularity with every book he wrote by overdoing himself, and that he never knew when he had said enough, from the appearance of his first volume of *Poems* (1851) to his last novel, *The Amazing Marriage* (1895).[16] It is true that certain patterns can be always traced in Meredith's novels, but once character is closely examined the common feature of this pattern through which character is first presented to us becomes gradually superfluous and character can no longer be fully interpreted in this light. At the same time sympathetic criticism which in giving close examination of character isolates a certain 'frame of feeling' and sets characters in it overlooks the individuality of character. An example of this occurs in a study by Joseph E. Kruppa in which he views the protagonists of the last three novels through what he calls thematic interrelationships. Kruppa sees that Victor as well as Ormont and Fleetwood treat their female partners as things rather than accepting them as independent consciousnesses. He shows that tragedy is brought about by their failure to achieve 'that mutual meetings of selves'.[17]

Such criticism—disparaging or otherwise—often leads to over-simplification, and it is with the intention of avoiding the tendency to oversimplify that I have devoted rather detailed study to each individual novel and its protagonist, making as little comparison between novels and their characters as possible. At the same time I have chosen the novels which share a common ground in order to show that Meredith could write an essentially different novel although on a similar theme. This brings us to the question posed by W. J. Lucas to Andre Gomme as to which novel should be read. If it is *The Egoist* (representing Meredith at his best) then *The Amazing Marriage* ought to be read along with it to see whether the choice is representative of Meredith at his worst or at his best, or whether it is representative at all. And if it is *Beauchamp's Career* which Gomme thought would do equally well, it is worthwhile to remember that Meredith reworked his political interest in greater depth in *One of Our Conquerors*. Or if *The Ordeal* be the greatest of Meredith's novels (as many admirers believe) then attention should be drawn to *Harry Richmond* so as to see the other side of the picture.

Meredith has a complex mind and it is unlikely that one novel, for better or worse reasons, would be sufficient to explore such complexity or the range of an output which extended over a span of forty years. The exclusion of Meredith from F. R. Leavis's 'great tradition' may in fact prove of benefit to Meredith's reputation: a writer such as Meredith, whose full range and complexity can only be appreciated from reading him *in extenso*, could hardly have been fitted without distortion into a tradition to which no novelist is admitted on the strength of more than one particular novel.

Appendix I: A Note on Susanne Howe's *Wilhelm Meister and his English Kinsmen: Apprentices to Life*

Susanne Howe's study (*Wilhelm Meister and his English Kinsmen, Apprentices to Life*, Columbia University Press, 1930) is certainly informative, particularly in connection with Goethe's influence on those English writers who seemed to have taken *Wilhelm Meister* as the archetype of the *Bildungsroman*. This study (which seems to have excluded major English novelists and their practice of the autobiographical form) shows that the genre was known to English readers early in the century, especially after Carlyle's translation of *Wilhelm Meister* (1824).

Wilhelm Meister evidently attracted the attention of contemporary writers, who tried to adapt it for their own purposes. They were, however, influenced by Carlyle's interpretation of Goethe's intentions, in particular by his understanding of *Entsagen* as self-denial. Fiction-writers of the time in obedience to this conviction constructed intricate plots with incidents which often lead to the punishment of the protagonist when he falls short of self-denial.

Bulwer-Lytton, for example, reveals serious interest in *Wilhelm Meister*, both in his essays and in his fiction. In his essays 'On the Departure of Youth', 'The Knowledge of the World in Men and Books' and 'On Satiety', he emphasises the importance of experience in education. In the last essay he says: 'Experience is not acquired by the spectator of life, but by its actor. It was not by contemplating the fortunes of others, but by the resemblance of his own, that the wisest of mortals felt that "All is vanity". A true and practical philosophy, not of books alone, but of mankind, is acquired by the passions as well as by the reason.'[1] On several occasions he acknowledges the direct influence of *Wilhelm Meister*. This influence is, however, tempered by the Carlylean view, with the result that moral principles direct the course of his apprentice protagonist's education. In *Pelham* (1828) the protagonist seeks a moral conquest of the world by becoming 'a disciple of Wisdom'. *The Disowned* (1829), Bulwer-Lytton says, is concerned 'to personify certain dispositions influential upon conduct, and to trace, . . . through the dark windings of Vice, which is Ignorance— through the broad course of Virtue, which is Wisdom—the various channels in which the grand principles of human conduct pour their secret but unceasing tide.'[2] More details of his plan are to be found in the long allegorical 'Introduction' to the book. The 1852 edition appears with an advertisement saying that the author, at the time of writing, 'was deeply engaged in the study of metaphysics and ethics—and out of that study grew the character of Algernon Mordaunt'.

The preface to the 1840 edition of *Ernest Maltravers* (1837) makes his debt to *Wilhelm Meister* explicit as he summarises the purpose of the book: 'For the original idea, which, with humility, I will venture to call the philosophical design, of a moral education or apprentice-ship, I have left it easy to be seen that I am indebted to Goethe's "Wilhelm Meister." But, in "Wilhelm Meister", the apprenticeship is rather that of the theoretical art. In the more homely plan that I set before myself, the apprenticeship is that of practical life.'[3]

The contrasting of the theoretical and the practical reflects a contemporary preoccupation of English writers, variously ex-pressed as the tension between the ideal and the real, romance and realism—a preoccupation which perhaps made the *Bildungsroman* appealing to the writers of the time. Disraeli, who also found the apprenticeship novel a useful genre, expressed his awareness of this tendency in a letter to Sarah Disraeli: 'In *Vivian Grey* I have portrayed my active and real ambition. In *Alroy* my ideal ambition. The Psychological Romance [*Contarini Fleming*] is a development of my poetic character. The trilogy is the secret history of my feelings.'[4]

In an attempt to demonstrate the 'active and real', Disraeli provides Vivian with an adventurous career, but in describing his flight to Germany following involvement in a duel, Disraeli drifts into the popular practice of sensational fiction. Vivian's adventures in Germany recall Harry's in *Harry Richmond*. Like the Professor, Dr Julius von Karsteg in *Harry Richmond*, Beckendorff, the Prime Minister of Reisenberg, acts as a mentor to the protagonist. He instructs Vivian: 'Fate, Destiny, Chance, particular and special Providence; idle words! Dismiss them all, sir! A man's fate is his own temper; and according to that will be his opinions as to the particular manner in which the course of events is regulated.'[5] This pronouncement is in accordance with the design of the book where the hero is doomed to failure because his ambition is not controlled by moral principles. Disraeli declares that he is already aware of the end Vivian will come to, as he can only see tragic failure awaiting vain ambitious youth.[6]

Thus the original design of *Wilhelm Meister* as a quest for self-knowledge seems to have remained inaccessible to the pioneer and his followers who exploited the genre in their own way. The reviews of the time did not give Goethe and *Wilhelm Meister* a good reception.[7] It was not until G. H. Lewes wrote *The Life and Works of Goethe* (1855) that Goethe was given prominence as an artist. In his study Lewes is concerned to dismiss the search for moral judgements in *Wilhelm Meister*: 'I take it to mean that in *Wilhelm Meister* there is a complete absence of all "moral verdict" on the part of the author. Characters tread the stage, events pass before our eyes, things are done and thoughts are expressed; but no word comes from the author respecting the moral bearing of these things. Life forgets in activity all moral verdict.'[8]

However Lewes fails to put theory into practice and he is unable to avoid moral verdict. In *Ranthorpe*, which draws heavily upon Goethe and *Wilhelm Meister*, the core of the book is moral, and Ranthorpe emerges from his apprenticeship as defined by his struggle to benefit the world. The same effect is conveyed in Lewes's incomplete novel, *The Apprenticeship of Life*.

With Charles Dickens the *Bildungsroman* gains firm ground. In his achievement Dickens neither resorts to the German source of the genre nor falls back on the moral strain of duty which prevailed in the novels of the time. In her study (referred to earlier) Susanne Howe curiously omits all reference to Dickens.

David Copperfield (1850), Dickens's first attempt in this field, invokes the main characteristics of the *Bildungsroman*. It is first a record of the narrator's 'written memory' of his own experience as David says.[9] As Q. D. Leavis acutely commented, Dickens started to write the novel after he had abandoned his autobiography project, 'because he *did* want to examine *impersonally* the experience of growing up in the first half of the 19th century, with the problems that a young man of that generation incurred, an examination needing the kind of objectivity that inheres in the novelist's art, but still one best exposed through the autobiographical form.'[10] This comment is, I think, an appropriate description of the *Bildungsroman*.

Appendix II: An Assessment of Margaret Tarratt's 'The Adventures of Harry Richmond – Bildungsroman and Historical Novel'

In her study 'The Adventures of Harry Richmond—Bildungsroman and Historical Novel' Margaret Tarratt 'intend[s] to show that Harry Richmond bears a closer affinity to Wilhelm Meister and the German Bildungsroman than to any contemporary English 'autobiographical' novels. At the same time, it is not a mere imitation of such a genre, but an interpretation and comment in terms that are related to the state of British society and the dilemma of the young Englishman looking for a field of relevant action' (Meredith Now, p. 166).

The parallel Margaret Tarratt makes between the Goethean Bildungsroman and Meredith's Harry Richmond is useful. For example, she relates the Princess Ottilia in Harry Richmond to Goethe's Schone Seele, and makes a parallel between Harry's rejection of his father's and grandfather's schemes, and Wilhelm's turning away from the commercial career prepared for him. Wilhelm, as well as Harry, she soundly remarks, is after a course of self-cultivation, and this is what essentially characterises them both as Bildungsroman heroes.

However, Margaret Tarratt's findings have general rather than particular bearings on Harry Richmond.

Her comparison remains inadequate. Margaret Tarratt raises an important point, for example, when she refers to Goethe's Elective Affinities, which occurs in Meredith's letter to Maxse. (p. 170) But this point receives no elaboration. The division in Harry's self against itself or against the world (which in general terms come close to Goethe's Elective Affinities) is a main aspect in Harry's life. One half of Harry finds its affinity in Janet, the other in Ottilia, and when

Janet and Ottilia meet, Harry feels that the division in him is, temporarily at least, healed.

The division in the self is a main preoccupation in Meredith's thought, and though it comes close to the Goethean ideas of polarity and enhancement, it is never developed on a similar complex level as that in which Goethe uses his scientific knowledge. Meredith merely dabbles in a kind of chemical organisation of character when he presents Fleetwood in *The Amazing Marriage*.

On the other hand the parallel that Margaret Tarratt makes between the Ottilie of *Elective Affinities* and that of *Harry Richmond* (p. 170) may be far fetched. Meredith's Ottilia (if the search for a parallel is necessary) bears as much resemblance to Ottilie's niece, Charlotte, as to Ottilie herself. In my study I have deliberately avoided reference to the *Elective Affinities* because the complex feelings of fear, suspicion and jealousy that exist between the aunt and the niece have no significant parallel in Meredith's novel. Even when it happens that Meredith draws upon a scene from the *Elective Affinities* he develops it differently. This is particularly noticeable in the lake scene between Harry and Ottilia, which is presumably derived from a similar scene in the *Elective Affinities*. In *Harry Richmond* the scene acquires a different and, at the same time, simpler emotional setting altogether.

Thus I have limited my reference to *Wilhelm Meister* because it is closer to *Harry Richmond* than the *Elective Affinities*; at the same time I have limited my reference to the general rather than specific characteristics of the Goethean *Bildungsroman*, though I do not agree that Meredith's contribution is mainly related to his extending the German frontiers of the genre to history instead of being limited to self-cultivation. It is here that the main difference lies between Margaret Tarratt's approach to *Harry Richmond* and mine.

Margaret Tarratt sees that the 'contrast of national character-istics is an important feature of *Harry Richmond*'. (p. 168) She then remarks that the framework for Harry's aspiration 'is initially a conventional one of patriotism'. (p. 173) On Harry's university education she comments that 'although he studies voluntarily at a German university, he is completely out of his element in the contest of the intellectual life shared by Ottilia and Professor von Karsteg'. (p. 173)

In my opinion the theme of national characteristics is a side issue in the book. It is Meredith's habit to raise various comments on English life. He perhaps realised that such comments were irrelcvant when he thought of suppressing them from the first revised edition (1886).

Harry's university education in Germany is not essentially intended to provide him with a different culture but rather to train him intellectually, and to enable him to grasp the totality of education by experience and, at the same time, to help him go beyond speculation.

The fact that Harry's education here comes from a German Princess and a German Professor of a German university should not, I think, lead to the assumption that Harry's aim is to test German culture versus English culture. Harry would have met a similar Ottilia and a similar Professor von Karsteg if, instead, he had happened to go up to Oxford or Cambridge. Professor von Karsteg comes closer to Dr Shrapnel in *Beauchamp's Career* than to any figure in *Wilhelm Meister*.

Harry's university education provides him with the independence of mind which is essential for the *Bildungsroman* hero. It bears fruit as Harry in later maturity becomes capable of seeing through life independent of his ties.

In viewing the union between Harry and Janet, a triumph of the real (national characteristics) over the ideal (foreign characteristics) would limit the range of conflict in Harry to the dilemma of belonging, which I consider only an overt theme in Harry's quest for education.

In my study I have tried to demonstrate that Harry's final union with Janet suggests no moral triumph of the real over the ideal; rather that the choice between them is a complex matter. Love is as much of a delusion as life itself, Harry says on one occasion (XXXVIII, 434), and Harry's sensibility is shaped as much by his strivings for the ideal (Ottilia and the German life) as by his feelings towards the real (Janet and his or their home). The fact that Harry's separation from Ottilia sends 'the whole structure of my idea of my superior nature . . . crumbling into fragments', as Margaret Tarratt remarks (p. 175) suggests to me not a destruction of the original structure of the ideal but a reconstruction in the total structure of the ideal and real together. It is a reconstruction in a *finer tone* which may be described as the emergence of a new sensibility in Harry. It is demonstrated through Harry's and Ottilia's final awareness that it is courage (the irrational) and not reason (the rational) that had led to the resolution of the situation.

The ideal in Harry is not, as Margaret Tarratt remarks, the kind of performance where 'Meredith demonstrates the destructive quality of self-disgust which may issue from an over-wearied attempt to live up exalted expectations'. (p. 175) The quest for the ideal remains constantly determined by Harry's desire to know about the nature of the ideal even after he has realised the futility of his love for Ottilia in terms of marriage. I have tried to demonstrate this point by analysing the situation where Harry asks Ottilia what appeals to her in Janet. Harry's question obliquely suggests his desire to know why the ideal union between him and Ottilia remains short of achievement.

Harry is not a knight-errant, and his search for the ideal is different in nature from that of Richard and Beauchamp. In Richard, knight-errantry is a kind of dream which dominates his life until the end; so is knight-errantry in Beauchamp's early career which is characterised by hero-worship. In both knight-errantry is a mode of life which dominates adulthood as well as boyhood. It is here that the distinction between Harry and his predecessors can be made.

What Margaret Tarratt calls knight-errantry I tend to describe as romance which is, as I have shown, the vision of life grasped by the imagination of the boy Harry. Later in adulthood romance is transformed into a kind of ideal which expresses itself in Harry's desire to achieve a union with Ottilia. However, Harry's awareness of the ideal falling short of achievement does not reverse his attitude towards the ideal nor does it curb the vitality of his quest for education. It remains, then, a debatable matter whether 'Harry's choice of action at any given point is influenced by his own unravelling history' as Margaret Tarratt notices. (p. 177) The quotation from Harry Richmond which Margaret Tarratt uses in connection with man's fate expresses Harry's or his creator's tendency to generalise.

The will which Harry acquires in his maturity is the kind of power which allows him to accept whatever may happen rather than attempt to change what may be brought about by destiny, circumstances or, in Meredith's term by 'the action of fortunes'.

Margaret Tarratt's overemphasis on 'the social and even geographical setting' (p. 179) leads, I think, to the underestimation of the individual experience in the shaping of Harry's sensibility as he passes from childhood to maturity. For example, Margaret Tarratt misrepresents Harry's rejection of the actor in his father by making it a parallel to Wilhelm's rejection of the world of actors. (p. 177)

Such consideration overlooks the fact that Harry rejects the actor in his father only when his father intervenes by his analysis and interrupts the spontaneity of action. The emphasis here is on the contrast between the life of imagination in Harry and the world of adulthood (as represented by his father). It is not a conflict between Harry and society. In maturity, conflict, then, is in the divided self against itself or against the world at large. Margaret Tarratt tends to extend the range of conflict to society and makes of it a main partner. This, I think, results in the underestimation of the individual experience in the conflict. Margaret Tarratt soundly remarks that Meredith does not limit himself to the German or Goethean *Bildungsroman*, but without realising, however, that he extends his range of experience to what may be described as the English *Bildungsroman* rather than to the historical English background.

Appendix III:
On the Reception of
One of Our Conquerors by
Contemporary Reviews

Of the first group are the following reviews. The *Anti-Jacobin* sees either little or no distinction between *The Egoist* and *One of Our Conquerors* as regards the artistic excellences of the two books. 'Mr Meredith's new Book', the review goes on to say, 'is not only good art, but great art also; it is filled and alive with this intimate concern for human nature in that battle of circumstances which is the condition of social life.'[1] *The National Observer* is similarly general in its comment when it remarks that Meredith 'displays an epitome of essential human life; and the lessons we severally draw from *One of Our Conquerors* are merely the lessons we may severally draw at pleasure from human life itself. Which is one of the tests of true life.'[2] *The Academy* recommends a third or fourth reading of the book after which confusion will disappear and intelligibility will be reached. It justifies the union with Nataly and defends the marriage to Mrs Burman on the ground of the hero's relations with nature and society.[3]

The second group attempts a balanced consideration of the general merits and faults of the book. *The Daily Chronicle* remarks that 'Meredith grows more and more trying. That discare of compression, which made so much of Browning's later work artistically worthless, is more than ever his master in this new novel.' It quotes the first sentence of the book and comments: 'Surely the loyalty of a Le Gallienne even must be tried by such writing as this'. But the review defends Meredith's difficult style on the ground that a most daring theme such as that which he chooses demands a robust treatment. It recommends patience and a certain effort on the part of the reader to achieve any reward.[4] *Vanity Fair* traces a correspondence between *The Egoist* and *One of Our Conquerors*. It criticises the presence of Meredith's 'mannerism' in *One of Our Conquerors* but then notices that 'there is enough beauty to balance any mannerism possible to the writer of it.'[5] *The Speaker* concentrates on the difficulty of style, while acknowledging that this difficulty gradually disappears. It dwells in detail on syntax in Meredith and praises the death scene towards the end. Though it is not Meredith's best novel, the review concludes, the book 'is well worthy of him'.[6] *The Times* similarly criticises the difficult syntax. It then comments on the prevailing sense of pain communicated by the novel: 'Mr. Meredith's novels make the appeal through the sense of pain; but until an era of asceticism in amusement arrives, the penitential exercise of reading his works will never be really attractive to the generality of cultivated minds.' The review sees that the book still 'exhibits that unity of purpose without which no novel can be great, but which, taken alone, is not greatness'.[7] *The Athenaeum* comments favourably on Meredith's descriptive power of character and situation. At the same time it criticises his difficult style and particularly his phraseology. The review concludes by asking Meredith 'to allow the stream of his genius to flow a little less turbidly'.[8]

From the rest of the reviews *One of Our Conquerors* receives unanimous condemnation. Some of these reviews, for example, react strongly against the opening sentence of the book,[9] and they all comment on the difficulty of Meredith's style. As Meredith despises simplicity *The Daily Telegraph* thinks that he ought to be 'fit only for the lower herd of handicraftsmen, and not to be accepted among the shining ranks of the Olympians'. The *Glasgow Herald* sees no reason why the ordinary reader 'should willingly and wittingly undergo the ordeal of Mr. Meredith's style'. *The Daily News* considers 'the book a theme for variations after the manner of its author: that manner is now merely a style run to seed'. The review laments the loss of the story-teller's purpose amid the 'topical conceits, more or less remotely connected with plot, character and action'. The *Saturday Review* quotes the sentence about puzzles 'presented to us now and then in the course of our days . . .' (I, 34), commenting that 'this sentence is not only a fair sample of Mr. Meredith's style, but admirably describes the state of mind of the person who attempts to read through *One of Our Conquerors*'. The review finds Meredith's style provoking because the story is so simple that it can be told in three lines.

The *Manchester Guardian* also comments on Meredith's style and syntax. It refers to 'the soft complaint of the gentle lady who wondered why so good and clever a man as Mr. Meredith should grudge the reading of his beautiful books to poor people who know no tongue but English'.[10] *The Spectator* believes that the author disdains straightforward narrative, description and characterisation. 'While his characteristic merits are in abeyance', the review concludes, 'his characteristic defects are in evidence on every page.'[11]

The Pall Mall Gazette considers *One of Our Conquerors* inferior to all Meredith's previous achievements. It notices the author's failure to develop his inspiring theme with the consequence that his characters become mere shadows.[12]

However, *One of Our Conquerors* receives little attention even from admirers of Meredith. In his review 'The Genius of George Meredith', which is presumably about *One of Our Conquerors*, Richard Garnett casually refers to the book: 'The title of Mr. George Meredith's last work might pass for a compendious description of himself. He is indeed "one of our conquerors".' Garnett then observes that the Meredith who made Diana acceptable despite her outrageous act is capable of making another character similarly acceptable.[13] It is not surprising that M. B. Forman takes the review to be of Richard Le Gallienne's book on Meredith (1889).[14]

In his article 'Meredith for the Multitude' Le Gallienne comments that 'people who read nothing but the reviews of *One of Our Conquerors* face you with one of the gibbeted quotations'. Though Le Gallienne defends Meredith's difficult style and refers to some of the previous novels he maintains silence over *One of Our Conquerors* in this connection.[15] This suggests his dissatisfaction with it, as is confirmed by the postscript he later added to his study. In this postscript (1899) Le Gallienne remarks that *One of Our Conquerors* is the least satisfactory of Meredith's works published since 1890. He criticises its style: 'In fact, on the whole, it is the most irritating of all Mr. Meredith's books; it contains more crabbed phrasing and less felicities than any book Mr. Meredith wrote. The most impenetrable passages of *The Egoist* and *Diana* are lit by electric light compared with the average writing in *One of Our Conquerors*. Probably no book ever written has begun with an opening sentence so appallingly deterrent.' Le Gallienne quotes the sentence. as 'a curious example of diseased expression', presenting the reader, as he does so, with the same 'gibbeted quotation' he earlier criticised.[16]

Appendix IV:
On the Reception of
The Amazing Marriage by
Contemporary Reviews

The reviews which followed the appearance of the book gave diverse assessment of its narrative structure. *The Standard*, for example, praises Meredith's unusual directness, a quality which it sees lacking in his previous works.[1] *The Realm* remarks that 'everything, or everything of the least importance, is clearly conceived, clearly told'.[2] *The Saturday Review*, however, comments on the difficulty and peculiar individuality of Meredith's style, referring it to 'his method of telling his story indirectly, through the means of puppet proxies'.[3] *St. James Gazette* similarly remarks that 'Meredith's style has now reached such a pitch that it is difficult to enjoy and sometimes impossible to understand what he writes'.[4]

Similarly, with character and action, reviews vary in their critical opinion. *The Athenaeum* gives Meredith credit for explaining 'seemingly incongruous events and apparently irrational people by making them live'.[5] The *Publisher's Circular* observes that the characters of the book 'live and move and have their being, not as creatures of the imagination, but as veritable beings of flesh and blood'.[6] Meanwhile the *St. James Gazette* sees the characters as 'a crowd of mere shadowy personages', and *The Daily Telegraph* criticises the lack of straightforwardness in character.[7] *The Echo* thinks that Meredith 'makes his characters do the unexpected and the impossible thing' for an unworthy plot.

Reviews generally tend to judge the purpose of the book from only one of the aspects of the narrative and it is often the straightforward narrative which appeals most to reviewers. *The Pall Mall Gazette*, *The Bookman* and *The Morning* are motivated in their appreciation of the book by the easy flow of the narrative in the early chapters. They describe the book as a romance.

Modern critical judgement of the book is not very different from that of the Victorian reviews. Sassoon who, for example, quotes in appreciation some of these reviews, believes that the earlier chapters (the first eight) 'are full of gusto and freshness, which perceptively diminishes as the story progresses'. He quotes Meredith's remark in Chapter ix that ' "language became a flushed Bacchanal in a ring of dancing similes" ' as being suggestive of Meredith's later style. He particularly quotes Edmund Gosse's review which draws upon the gambling scene (ix, 97) commenting, that 'it was prominent in expressing a candid protest against the peculiarity of style which so many people have since found vexatious'. He notices that Meredith's 'loss of vitality only becomes obvious after the seventeenth chapter' where 'the writing begins to resemble *One of Our Conquerors*'.[8]

In the course of his discussion of the book and its relevance to previous novels Lionel Stevenson says that 'for the first time since *Harry Richmond* Meredith created an atmosphere of sheer romance'.[9] Walter Wright, on the other hand considers the book as an attempt where 'Meredith was contented with a simple contrast between romance and egoism or sentimentality.'[10]

Notes

CHAPTER 1

1. The subject was discussed in the front page article (25 Nov. 1960, pp. 749–50) after the *Delta* had devoted more than half of its October (1960) issue to the subject in question. Letters and replies by Gomme and Lucas commenting on the dispute appeared in the following numbers: 2 Dec., p. 779; 9 Dec., p. 797; 16 Dec., p. 813.
2. *Spectator* (Feb. 1866) p. 136.
3. For more details see the author's discussion 'Forster on Meredith', *The Review of English Studies*, XXIV (1973) pp. 185–91.
4. Christopher Caudwell in Samuel Hynes (ed.), *Romance and Realism: a Study in English Bourgeois Literature* (Princeton: 1970) p. 81.
5. David Daiches, *A Critical History of English Literature*, IV (1968) p. 1072.
6. Donald Fanger, 'George Meredith as Novelist', *Nineteenth Century Fiction*, XVI (1962) pp. 226–7. This view can be found in S. M. Ellis's study: *George Meredith: His Life and Friends in Relation to his Work* (1919).
7. V. S. Pritchett, *Introduction to The Egoist* (London: The Bodley Head, 1972) p. vi.
8. Gwendolyn O. Stewart, 'George Meredith, One of Our Conquerors' (Diss. Columbia, 1966) p. 13.
9. E. M. Forster, *Aspects of the Novel* (1968) p. 98.
10. George Meredith, *Westminster Review* (Apr. 1857) p. 616.
11. George Meredith, *Blue Notebook*. (Yale University Library).
12. W. J. Harvey, *Character and the Novel* (1966) pp. 74–100.
13. Walter Wright, *Art and Substance in George Meredith* (Nebraska, 1953) p. 159.
14. Donald Stone, *Novelists in a Changing World* (Harvard University Press, 1972) p. 119.
15. Gillian Beer, in Ian Fletcher (ed.), *Meredith Now* (1971) p. 268.
16. The phrase was used by D. H. Lawrence, *Collected Letters* (1962) p. 282.

CHAPTER 2

1. Lionel Stevenson, *The Ordeal of George Meredith* (New York: 1953) p. 59.
2. T. S. Eliot, *Selected Essays* (1932) p. 18.
3. This recalls Sidgwick's notion of egoism where the egoist views the rationale for judgements of praiseworthiness and blameworthiness or for judgements of personal worth and merit 'as a means of encouraging the production of future good, and preventing future harm, much as the utilitarian does.' (J. B.

Schneewind, *Sidgwick's Ethics and Victorian Moral Philosophy* (Oxford, 1977) p. 360.)

4. H. Spencer, 'Intellectual Education', *North British Review* (May 1854), 'Moral Education' and 'Physical Education', *British Quarterly Review* (April 1858 and April 1859); all were published in book form in 1861 under the title *Education*. In a later work (*The Study of Sociology* (1874) p. 402) Spencer says: 'As between infancy and maturity there is no shortcut by which there may be avoided the tedious process of growth and development through insensible increments; so there is no way from the lower forms of social life to the higher, but one passing through small successive modification.'

5. Herbert Spencer *Education* (1861) p. 118.

6. Ibid., p. 137.

7. Auguste Comte, *The Positive Philosophy*, I, translated by Martineau (London: 1853) pp. 12–13.

8. William Whewell, 'Of Art and Science' in *Philosophy of the Inductive Sciences* (1858) pp. 129–35. This collection first appeared in 1840. Its third edition (1858–60) is considerably enlarged, and it is significant for including the section on J. S. Mill, who, though he disputed his philosophy, benefited from both this collection and his earlier book: *History of the Inductive Sciences* (1837). The controversy between the two continued for several years, with Mill accusing Whewell of being a reactionary rationalist and Whewell criticising his opponent for his failure to establish hypothesis in practice. Whewell can be better described as standing for what is now known as the 'hypothetico-deductive' school in opposition to the proponents of the classical 'problem of induction'—which is still disputable. Whewell is, however, remembered for his pioneering effort to bridge the gap between arts and natural sciences which was a characteristic feature of the English educational system.

9. William Whewell, *Philosophy of the Inductive Sciences: On the Philosophy of Discovery, Chapters Historical and Critical* (1860; first published 1840) pp. 316–17.

10. Lukacs considers it very important that the character can generalise intellectually. 'Generalisation sinks to the level of empty abstraction only when the bond between abstract thought and the personal experiences of the character disappear, when we do not experience this bond together with him.' He emphasises 'the continuous experiencing of the vital connection between the characters' personal experience and their intellectual experience'. *International Literature*, VIII (1936) pp. 58–60.

11. In his essay 'The Intellectual Physiognomy of Literary Characters' Lukacs says: 'The created character can be significant and typical only if the artist succeeds in disclosing the manifold connections between the individual traits of his heroes and the objective general problems of his time, if the character himself experiences the most abstract problems of his time as his own individual problems that are a matter of life and death for him.' *International Literature*, VIII (1936) p. 58.

12. The narrative tone is sometimes confused by the uneasy effort to make a balance between two impulses. This is well demonstrated from the scene where Sir Austin is travelling in London on his way to visit Mr Thompson:

    Sir Austin entered the great City with a sad mind. The memory of his misfortune came upon him vividly, as if no years had intervened, and it were but yesterday that he found the letter telling him that he had no wife, and his son no mother. He wandered on foot through the streets the first night of his arrival, looking strangely at the shops, and shows, and bustle of the World from which he had divorced himself; feeling as destitute as the poorest vagrant. He had almost forgotten how to find his way about, and came across his old mansion in his efforts to regain his hotel. The windows were alight; signs of merry life within. He stared at it from the shadow of the opposite side. It seemed to him he was a ghost gazing upon his living past. And then the Phantom which had stood there mocking while he felt as other men—the Phantom now flesh and blood Reality seized and convulsed his heart, and filled its unforgiving crevices with bitter ironic venom. He remembered by the time reflection returned to him that it was Algernon, who had the house at his disposal, probably giving a card-party, or something of the sort. In the morning, too, he remembered that he had divorced the World to wed a System, and must be faithful to that exacting Spouse, who, now alone of things on earth, could fortify and recompense him. (XIX, 118–19)

13. Critics have commented variously on Adrian's character. J. W. Beach, for example, views him as 'the low-minded and cynical Adrian Harley' with whom Sir Austin, he thinks, shares views of women. (*The Comic Spirit in George Meredith* (New York, 1911) p. 38).

A more popular critical assessment of Adrian's character is that of F. D. Curtin, who, in his approach, draws upon Meredith's theory of comedy as expressed in his *Essay*. 'The comic spirit, according to Meredith in his lecture, attempts to touch and kindle the mind through laughter, "to extinguish [folly] at the outset". Such a spirit pervades three quarters at least of *The Ordeal of Richard Feverel*' ('Adrian Harley: The Limits of Meredith's Comedy', *Nineteenth Century Fiction*, VII (1953) p. 274). Curtin believes that Meredith sets a limit for comedy in his fiction but not in his *Essay*, and that in *The Ordeal of Richard Feverel* Adrian helps the author to fix that limit clearly. He thinks that the book is dominated by comedy until the last quarter where Lady Blandish takes over from Adrian, when 'the tone shifts from·comedy to tragedy'. Such criticism denies the unique position of Adrian's comedy in Meredith's writing.

In the gallery of Meredith's comic figures Adrian is the most original creation. He is free from the dominion of the Comic Spirit, and he neither directs nor is directed by it. The corrective power which forms the basis of Meredith's theory of comedy does not apply to him, for Adrian lacks the ambition to correct Sir Austin's character, or Richard's, or even to achieve the 'happy balance' of comedy in his own life. He accepts 'humanity as it had been, and was'.

14. *Westminster Review*, XI (1857) p. 615.
15. G. L. Griest, *Mudie's Circulating Library and the Victorian Novel* (Indiana: 1971) p. 222.
16. Frank Kermode, *The Sense of an Ending* (1966) p. 30.
17. Robert Sencourt, *The Life of George Meredith*, p. 55.
18. Edward Clodd, *Memories* (1916) p. 146.
19. Justin McCarthy, 'Novels with a Purpose', *Westminster Review* (July 1864) p. 32.

20. It may be suggested here that Lady Judith's feeling against 'the army' reflects a current popular reaction to the Crimean War.
21. Knight-errantry takes a tragic turn when its effect is extended to Lucy, and this is where the source of tragedy can be traced. Phyllis Bartlett convincingly, I think, finds the origin of Richard's love for Lucy in that of Meredith for Mary. She argues that the knight-errant motive is the common ground for the tragic consequence of action. ('Richard Feverel, Knight-Errant', *Bulletin of the New York Public Library* (July 1859) pp. 329–40.)
22. Arnold Kettle, in Ian Fletcher (ed.), *Meredith Now*, p. 203.
23. Richard Sencourt, *The Life of George Meredith*, p. 64.

CHAPTER 3

1. Once Meredith commented that 'Goethe's "Wilhelm Meister" should give way to the volume of his "Gedichte" ' (*Letters*, III, p. 1503). On various occasions Meredith expressed his admiration for Goethe (see particularly *Letters*, I, p. 161; III, p. 1556).
   One may assume that Meredith's first acquaintance with *Wilhelm Meister* goes back to his early days of marriage with Mary Ellen as a correspondence between Mary and Hogg may reveal. This is what Hogg writes to Mary: 'Speaking of the Poetry of Life, I am now reading *Wilhelm Meister* for the third time, and with increased delight. . . . Pray find [the *unwritten* books of Wilhelm Meister] among Herculanean Papyri, or Palimpsest M.S.S. Since you are such a clever girl pray find them for me; and publish them, so that I may have a *new* volume every two, or three, months for the remainder of my life.' (Winifred Scott, *Jefferson Hogg* (1951), p. 249.)
2. Stephen Wall (ed.), *Charles Dickens* (1970) p. 155.
3. Richard Sencourt, *The Life of George Meredith*, p. 169.
4. For Meredith the 1860s was a period of great anxiety. Meredith experimented with sensational fiction mainly with the hope of achieving popularity.
5. In an earlier version of the letter as printed by W. M. Meredith the full stop at the end of the sentence is replaced by 'and', whereas the letter in the *MS* which I examined reads as above. The error made by the substitution confused many scholars of Meredith, such as M. B. Forman, M. Galland, and R. G. Sencourt who assumed that the letter refers to a lost autobiography or an autobiographic tale. In a more recent study of Meredith (in *Meredith Now*, p. 166) Margaret Tarrat made the same mistake by using the earlier version of the letter.
   It was Richard H. Hudson who first discovered the error and corrected it from the original in his study 'Meredith's Autobiography and "The Adventures of Harry Richmond" '. (*Nineteenth Century Fiction*, IX (1954) pp. 38–49).
6. He writes: 'My novel *Harry Richmond* is out of my hands, and appears in the Cornhill the 1st October [actually it began in September]'. (I, 420)
7. Original manuscript notes for a dramatic dialogue, synopses of scenes, outline of the chapters of a story, epigrams, anecdotes, etc. in *Altschul Collection*, Beinecke Rare Book and Manuscript Library of Yale University (1937). Other references to the sketch are all to this source.
8. Particular attention is drawn to an unpublished summary of a novel called

Mighty Society kept in the original manuscript notes. . . . The summary reads as follows:

Mighty Society (Novel)
A young fellow of good connections
Marries a splendid beauty of bourgeois family
She jilts a couple of suitors

She has a thirst for fashionable societies
Will do anything to enter them
Her husband compelled to spend beyond income
At last he forges to pay debts she contracted.

The secret of it known to one or two
They conceal it for a time—debate—

One vol.

A lawyer (Turdale, has a daughter to whom young Montagu is partly engaged before he marries the above. He discovers the forgery. The daughter in an interview with her father (he suspected her to be still in love with this man and telling her of the circumstances to cure her passion urges him to Montagu and declares she is ready to marry her father's nominee and gladly. The wife, wanting a divorce, threatens her husband before the lawyer; charges him with crime.

9. The scene is very reminiscent of the puppet show in *Wilhelm Meister*, where Wilhelm acts David and Goliath to the delight of the family and neighbours.
10. The tales of *The Arabian Nights* fit properly in David's boyhood mind and sensibility. David turns to *The Nights* as he spontaneously wishes to transform the concrete world of reality into a dream. The result is a fusion of the two worlds. David imagines Mr Peggotty's house Aladdin's palace while he and Ham are approaching the place. (I, 35) A similar analogy is established as David (in the company of Miss Mills) is going to Dora's house. (II, 56)
     David put Mr and Miss Murdstone into the bad characters of the fiction he read such as those of *The Arabian Nights* and the *Tales of the Genii*. In the meantime David identifies himself with the good ones. (I, 66) He similarly looked on Mr Jack Maldon as a modern Sinbad. (I, 290)
     Both David and Steerforth had a joint effort of entertainment by telling stories in the fashion of *The Arabian Nights*. (I, 111)
11. The sea imagery, as Barbara Hardy shows in her study of *Harry Richmond* (*The Appropriate Form: An Essay on the Novel* (1964) pp. 83–105) plays an important role in expressing the meaning of the book.
12. See 'The Battle of Dorking: Reminiscences of a Volunteer' *Blackwood's Magazine*, cix (1871) pp. 539–72.
13. In his portrayal, Roy is reminiscent of many of Meredith's other characters. Like Sir Austin, he schemes for his son's happiness, and Harry himself realises that 'father was never insincere in emotion'. (LIII, 636) Unlike Sir Austin, however, Roy's love for his son is not confused with egoism; hence the congruity between motive and action in his life. He is as consistent as Sir Austin is inconsistent.

The comic element in Roy, like that in Adrian, does not conform to Meredith's idea of comedy as described in the *Essay*. But, unlike Adrian, Roy is not detached from his action. As a comic character Roy is more straight-forward, and is void of sarcasm and irony.

In his quest for wealth and power, Roy resembles Victor in *One of Our Conquerors*. Both do their utmost to achieve wealth and power which is not theirs by birth. Roy's aspirations, however, for the highest position in the land, are unrelated to the current social situation which Victor struggles with. Comedy, rather than politics, is dominant in this aspect of Roy's scheming.

Roy's character has been more distinctly recognised, whether in praise or condemnation, than any other character in the book. Current reviewers judged it not on the moral basis of his pretensions, but on its vitality, and modern critics appreciate the character on its own merit. Within the context of the novel as a whole, however, reviewers have overestimated the countinuous revelation of comedy and romance in Roy, at the expense of underestimating the interaction of the histories of father and son, and Harry's emergence from romance.

Roy is as much set in his life as Harry is evolving. Like Wilhelm, Harry becomes estranged from his mentor. Harry's disillusionment is complete when he realises that his father 'clearly could not learn from misfortune'. (XLVII, 541) He is detached from the spell-binding hold which Roy had over him, and can see that 'to the rest of the world, he was a progressive comedy': nevertheless, his own love for his father enables him to see the tragedy of his 'unteachable spirit'. Thus, Harry's relationship with his father is clarified and acknowledged, enabling Harry to act appropriately in response to new demands of thought and feeling.

14. Like Natalie in *Wilhelm Meister*, Ottilia tends to like short expressions. She is reminiscent of the Princess Leonora, whose picture inspires G. H. Lewes to remark: 'It is by what she says, not what she does, that we know her; and though all she says is tinged with a pensive tenderness, and a sweet serenity of soul, we do not see her in action of the kind to reveal the individuality of her nature. Tasso (the protagonist of the poem) sees in her the ideal of feminine grace.' *Female Characters of Goethe from the Original Drawings of William Kaulbach with Explanatory Text* by G. H. Lewes (1867) p. 14.

15. An example on this occurs in L. T. Hergenhan's Introduction to *The Adventures of Harry Richmond* (University of Nebraska Press, 1970) p. xxvi.

16. Harry's remark about not loving the two at once does not seem to have been effective enough to divert the attention of contemporary reviewers, who condemned him on the basis of moral behaviour. The *Daily Telegraph* (20 Nov. 1871, p. 3), for example, notices that 'The hero, Harry Richmond, is a poor fellow indeed—feeble, inconsistent, made to be fallen in love with by every girl he meets. . . . One cannot but marvel how he won the heart of Janet, or retained that of Princess Ottilia; for both are infinitely above him in character and in all the best quality of heart.' The *Spectator* comments on the 'uncomfortable complexities of inconsistent obligation' in the hero's life. Wilhelm similarly was condemned by the reviewers on much the same grounds: 'And these passions not merely succeed each other with rapidity, but are often all upon him at once.' (*The London Magazine*, X (1824) p. 306) *The Monthly Review* comments on Wilhelm's shifting acquaintance (CVI (1825)

p. 528). *The Blackwood's Edinburgh Magazine* finds him 'altogether fanciful in his habits of mind, and absurd and irresolute in his conduct and demeanour' despite his enthusiastic youth of genius, amiability and modesty (xv (1924) p. 623). *Atlantic Monthly* criticises Wilhelm's oscillation, but justifies it on the basis of its evolving nature. (xvi (1865) p. 278)

17. This practice is very similar to that of Estella and Pip. Estella's penetration into Pip's inner life helps him realise his shortcomings. In her study of *Great Expectations* Q. D. Leavis remarks that 'The immediate effect of his acceptance of Estella's view of himself is to start being worthier of her by self-education and self-improvement'. (*Dickens the Novelist*, p. 299)

18. Quoted by G. H. Lewes in *The Life and Works of Goethe*, II (1855) p. 204.

19. The chapters deleted appear in the third volume of the first edition (1871) under the following titles and numbers: 'Janet and I', xiv; 'Janet's Heroism', xv; 'My Subjection', xvi.

   Two reasons might have led Meredith to make the revisions: one is his concern with the proportional emphasis on the acts of fortune and acts of mind. At this stage the narrative acts of fortune rather than of mind are needed to resolve the plot. The second reason may be related to the question of proportional balance of dramatic and narrative—with the deletion of the three chapters, the dramatised situation between Harry and Janet is mostly suppressed.

   More details about the revisions of *Harry Richmond* are in Hergenhan's 'Meredith's Revisions of *Harry Richmond*', *Review of English Studies* xiv (1963) pp. 24–32.

20. The text of this quotation and the one which follows are suppressed from the revised edition which first came out in 1886. Page reference in the two quotations is to vol. III of the first edition (*The Adventures of Harry Richmond*, 3 vols, 1871).

   Harry's revelation recalls Wilhelm's confession, where he retrospectively reflects on his past experience of love affairs:

   '. . . confess it thou lovest her [Natalia]; thou once more feelest what it means to love with thy soul. Thus did I love Mariana, and deceive myself so dreadfully; I loved Philina, and could not help despising her. Aurelie I respected, and could not love: Therese I reverenced, and paternal tenderness assumed the form of an affection for her. And now when all the feelings that can make a mortal happy meet within my heart, now am I compelled to fly! . . . Happier are they who strive for earthly wares!' (*Thomas Carlyle's Works*, vol. viii, Standard Edition, 1904, book viii, ch. vii, p. 123)

21. Here Harry reaches Wilhelm's conclusion: 'It avails not for mortals to complain of Fate or of themselves'. (*Thomas Carlyle's Works*, ibid., p. 155)

22. Norman Kelvin *A Troubled Eden*, p. 79.

23. Change in conclusion, however, is part of the alteration in the end Dickens decided to make 'from and after Pip's return to Joe's, and finding his little likeness there'. John Forster, *The Life of Charles Dickens*, II, p. 289.

24. It may be interesting to notice that Meredith saw an actual scene of fire while he was still engaged on *Harry Richmond*, and described it in a letter to John Morley (27 Jan. 1870):

The drama of a household burnt out under my eye here, has given me some excitement. Irish Mr Sewell, six feet five, haired like Erebus, brawny as Vulcan's first forgeman, with a sniffling English wife, whose shawl is, like her nose, always thawing off her shoulder, and a family of four, a good honest lot for that matter, lived in a hut in the corner of a field abutting on our acres, to watch potatoes grow. Sewell was away at work, his wife sniffling somewhere, when out flaps the big girl with a whinny, Fire! Fire!—and I giving a touch to *Richmond*. (1, 415)

25. In the *MS* this passage occurs in the margin of page 24—which obviously suggests that it was added as an afterthought.

CHAPTER 4

1. Edward Clodd, *Memories* (1916) p. 146.
2. 'Talks with George Meredith', *The National Review*, CXXXI (1948) p. 454.
3. Barbara Hardy, 'Introduction' in *The Appropriate Form* (1964) pp. 1–10.
4. See Kenneth Graham, *English Criticism of the Novel 1865–1900* (1965) pp. 34–8.
5. Bertrand Russell, *A Journal of the History of Ideas*, I (1940) p. 33.
6. Ibid., p. 25.
7. See Carlyle's admiration for George Fox's heavenly aspirations and earthly independence in *Sartor Resartus* (book III, chapter 1). All references to Carlyle's works are to the Centenary Edition (unless otherwise stated).
8. *Critical Miscellaneous Essays*, IV, p. 24.
9. Eugene Goodheart, *The Cult of the Ego* (Chicago: 1968) p. 78.
10. References are to the Standard Edition of *The Works of George Eliot* (Edinburgh: 1895).
11. Barbara Hardy (ed.), *Critical Essays on George Eliot* (1970) p. 104.
12. In her confession (as a result of offending Shrapnel and consequently Beauchamp), Rosamund realises that 'cowardice is the chief evil in the world' (XLVIII, 556).
13. See 'Our Novels. The Sensational School', *Temple Bar* (June 1870) pp. 419–20.
    'Light Literature', *Belgravia* (May 1873) p. 331.
14. See for example, *Saturday Review* (May 1866) p. 616; and *The Times* (18 Aug. 1876) p. 4.
15. Trollope, *My Confidence* (1896) p. 334.
16. Most of George Eliot's critical views appear in *Westminster Review* and *The Leader*. On one occasion she defines realism as 'the doctrine that all truth and beauty are to be attained by a humble and faithful study of nature, and not by substituting vague forms, bred by imagination on the mists of feeling, in place of definite, substantial reality'. (*Westminster Review* (Apr. 1856) p. 626) 'The Natural History of German Life' and 'Silly Novels by Lady Novelists', which appeared in the same journal and the same year, are two examples of her doctrine of the real.
17. *English Criticism of the Novel 1865–1900*, p. 27.
18. *Examiner* (8 January 1876) pp. 45–6.

19. *Pall Mall Gazette* (5 February 1876) p. 11.
20. *British Quarterly Review* (April 1879) p. 419.
21. Walter Wright, *Art and Substance in George Meredith*, pp. 102–27; Norman Kelvin, *A Troubled Eden*, pp. 83–100; V. S. Pritchett, *George Meredith and English Comedy*, pp. 99–112.
22. From *Original manuscript notes for a dramatic dialogue, synopsis of scenes, outline of the characters of a story, epigrams, anecdotes, etc.*, in *Altschul Collection*, preserved at the Beineke Rare and MSS Book Library of Yale University.
23. Jack Lindsay, *George Meredith* (1953) p. 205.
24. Lindsay assumes that the weakness in Beauchamp's character comes indirectly to Meredith through Maxse. But the model in Meredith is not, I think, a simple matter. Maxse's views on 'Woman's Suffrage', for example, are reactionary. Beauchamp's are the opposite. At the same time, Maxse's views on other issues, as published in the seventies, are progressive enough. He attacks Herbert Spencer's doctrine of self-help when he discusses 'National Education'. In his *The Causes of Social Revolt* (1872), Maxse sees the contradiction in Carlyle when he remarks that Carlyle, who 'is the most powerful calumniator of democracy, is also the great apostle of Kingship, force, oppression, and servility, does homage to what he calls the heaven-born docility of man' (p. 28). This recalls Meredith's independence of Carlyle's heroism. But Meredith has his own view of Carlyle. On one occasion he writes to Maxse: 'Carlyle preaches work for all to all. Good. But his method of applying his sermon to his "nigger" is intolerable. —Spiritual light he has to illuminate a nation. Of practical little or none, and he beats his own brains out with emphasis.' (I, 412)
    In his criticism, Lindsay tends to underestimate the fact that character in Meredith may and can invalidate a theory or a model in life.
25. *National Education and its Opponents: a Lecture by Rear-Admiral Maxse* (1877) p. 20.
26. Meredith would similarly say about *Beauchamp's Career* what he had said about *Harry Richmond* (in a letter to his friend Dr Jessopp), that he would leave the divine to Doctors of Divinity and deal with men and women of mortal lives (I, 451).
27. Jack Lindsay, op. cit., p. 212.
28. An account of the situation to which Beauchamp would belong comes in *Karl Marx and Frederick Engels on Britain* (Moscow: 1953) pp. 499–500.
29. Despite its critical appreciation *The Saturday Review* sees the tragic end as lacking in heroism: 'He is drowned in trying to save another's life, but this other is not the heroine, nor indeed any character with a place in the story, but a nameless little urchin who had fallen out of a boat in Southampton Water' (13 May 1876, p. 627). *The Academy* expresses its dissatisfaction with the ending and recommends its suppression. (16 Jan. 1876, p. 51) The highly appreciative *Canadian Monthly* was 'provoked for the time at the improbabilities in the dénouement'. (Apr. 1876, p. 343)
30. Albert J. LaValley, *Carlyle and the Idea of the Modern* (New Haven: Yale University Press, 1968) p. 246.
    For Carlyle's indestructibility of hero-worship see *Essays* IV, p. 24.
31. Clodd, pp. 148–9.

CHAPTER 5

1. The Ode was first published in *Macmillan's Magazine* (Apr. 1887) p. 405.
2. H. G. Wells, *The Story of a Great Schoolmaster* (1924) pp. 10–12.
3. A. Vizetelly, preface to Emile Zola, *Money* (1894) p. vi.
4. For more of Meredith's views on the political scene see 'Mr George Meredith on the Future of Liberalism. Home Rule and Imperialism', being an interview published in the *Manchester Guardian* (2 Feb. 1903) p. 5.
   See also his interview with W. T. Stead in *Review of Reviews*, xxix (1904) pp. 225–30 where Meredith shows his intense scorn for imperialism and 'regards the Empire as a mere flaunting feather in its cap'. The original complete version of the interview is edited by Joseph O. Baylen and Patrick G. Hogan in *Tennessee Studies in Literature*, ix (1964) pp. 99–116.
5. The letter is preserved in the Library of King's College, Cambridge, and does not appear in any collection of Meredith letters. E. M. Forster, *Letter Book*, ii.
6. The draft consists mainly of seventeen chapters: i–xvi and xix. For details about revisions see Frede Thomson, 'Stylistic Revisions of *One of Our Conquerors*' *Yale University Library Gazette*, xxxvi (1961) pp. 64–74. Meredith adopts the title 'A Conqueror of Our Time' until he reaches Chapter xv.
   In her study of Meredith (Diss. London University, 1969) Margaret Harris makes a detailed study of the two surviving drafts and speculates on the revision. Throughout the course of her study, she relates Victor's portrait to that of General Ople. In a previous study (*George Meredith, an Essay Towards Appreciation*, 1902, p. 159) Walter Jerrold similarly assumed that the title of the novel was derived from what Lady Camper says to her neighbour towards the end of the book. 'You would not have cared one bit for a caricature if you had not nursed the absurd idea of being one of our conquerors.' (viii, 185)
   It is an oversimplification, however, to consider Victor a type of conquering egoist such as General Ople and Willoughby who belong to those whom Meredith lists in his *Notebook* as 'The Conqueror of Hearts'.
7. Earlier in a poem *Lines to a Friend Visiting America* (1868) Meredith says:

> A false majority, by stealth,
> Have got her fast, and sway the rod:
> A headless tyrant built of wealth
> The hypocrite, the belly-God. (ii, 8)

8. *Letters of Henry James*, ii, selected and edited by Percy Lubbock (1920) p. 455.
9. Writing to his son Arthur (July 1881) Meredith says: 'I myself am, as a describer of nature and natural emotions, a constant sufferer in dealing with a language part of which is dead matter. —You will do good service in directing attention to the point, though I do not see how our English is to be vitalised throughout.' (ii, 632)
10. Arthur Symons, *Figures of Several Centuries* (1916) p. 141.
11. By 'society' Meredith means here the two points of exploitation: one belonging to the commercial expansion; the other to convention. Both exercise leadership in society. Meredith hints at such a society in *Diana of the Crossways* when he

says that it is 'a crazy vessel worked by a crew that formerly practised piracy, and now, in expiation, professes piety, fearful of a discovered Omnipotence, which is in the image of themselves and captain'. (xviii, 209) Another hint comes in a letter to Laurie Magnus when Meredith says that 'society is kept in animation by the customary, in the first place, and secondly by sentiment. It has little love of Earth (or Nature) and gives ear mainly to those who shiver with dreads of the things that are, not seeing that a frank acceptance of Reality is the firm basis of the Ideal.' (iii, 1618–19) Nature is the counterpower of change which helps establish a new order of leadership in society in place of the existing one. It is the aspiration of the non-expansionist and non-conventional individual to put the ideal into practice and make it real.

Victor cannot, for example, envisage society in its existing order to be 'in the dance with Nature' (xxxvi, 435) because of the conflict between the power of change and tradition.

12. Nataly's inaction seems to have prompted harsh judgement on her character. Garnet Smith (*The Fortnightly Review*, May 1896, p. 787) describes Nataly as being 'cowardly in not offering helpful dissuasive council to Victor'. He takes her as an expression of the 'subservient parasite', that is, of the contemporary woman Meredith intended to portray. Pelham Edgar ascribes Victor's persistent aims at social triumph to Nataly's timidity (*National Review*, September 1907, p. 78).

Bernard A. Richards similarly views Nataly as timid (in *Meredith Now* p. 292).

13. Ian Fletcher, *Meredith Now*, p. 275.

14. Jack Lindsay, op. cit., pp. 282–5.

15. Ibid., p. 297.

16. Perhaps Meredith's friend Henley would be a more appropriate candidate than Hyndman. In his passionate attachment to the Empire Henley seemed to find consolation for a personal tragedy. Meredith writes to the Earl of Plymouth (5 July 1907): 'Rightly could he [Henley] speak of his un-conquerable soul. It was a soul that had to do perpetual battle with an undermined and struggling body, and this joyfully, and, as far as could be possible, buoyantly; for all his nature sprang up to hail the divinity of life' (iii, 1599).

17. Jack Lindsay, op. cit., p. 298.

18. *The Historical Basis of Socialism in England* (1883) p. 430. For more details about Hyndman's views on Socialism see his *The Coming Revolution in England* (1884) and *The Social Reconstruction of England* (1884). See also Frederick J. Gould, *Hyndman, Prophet of Socialism* (1928), and C. Tsuzuki, *H. M. Hyndman and British Socialism* (Oxford, 1961).

19. See W. T. Stead's 'Interview with George Meredith', *Tennessee Studies in Literature*, p. 105.

20. Norman Kelvin, *A Troubled Eden*, pp. 172–3. Kelvin misrepresents Victor's inclination for 'good citizenship' (xiii, 137) by assuming that Victor 'though he defies society, is now lawless'. He fails to see that Victor considers himself lawless in relation to nature and not to society. This point is clarified earlier in the book in a discussion about 'Nature and the Institution of Man': 'But no; we may be rebels against our time and its Laws; if we are really for Nature, we are not lawless'. (xi, 120–1)

Kelvin's point is that Victor's defiance of society brings about tragedy. The same view was presented earlier by Pelham Edgar, who says that 'the difficulty [in *One of Our Conquerors*] is resolved when we realise that Victor Radnor wrecks his life by seeking to conquer a society whose laws he has defied' (George Meredith', *Northern Review*, September 1907, p. 80).

21. Oscar Wilde, *The Soul of Man under Socialism* (1919) p. 75.

CHAPTER 6

1. For more details of the drafts see the author's note 'On the MSS of *The Amazing Marriage*' *Notes and Queries*
2. Christopher Caudwell, *Romance and Realism*, p. 81.
3. Grant Allen and Meredith lived within visiting distance of each other, and they met and talked on several occasions. Clodd records Meredith's comment on Allen's novel as saying that 'The present marriage system [was] a failure, but its modification [was] not helped by manifestos of the type of [Grant Allen's] *The Woman Who Did*, which Meredith regards as lacking both novelty and Art' (*The Times Literary Supplement*, 8 May 1953, p. 308).
4. In his study of Ibsen, Edmund Gosse records that 'In April, 1879, it is understood, a story was told him of an incident in the Danish courts, the adventure of a young married woman in one of the small towns of Zealand, which set his thoughts running on a dramatic enterprise. He was still curiously irritated by contemplating, in his mind's eye, the "respectable, estimable narrow-mindedness and worldliness" of social conditions in Norway, where there was no aristocracy, and where a lower middle-class took the place of nobility, with, as he thought, sordid results.' (*Ibsen*, New York, 1907, p.157)

   In a letter to Edmund Gosse (July 1879) Ibsen wrote: 'I have been living here in Rome with my family since September, and have been keeping myself busy with a new dramatic work [*A Doll's House*] that will soon be finished in October. It is a serious play, really a domestic family drama, dealing with contemporary problems in regard to marriage.' (*Ibsen Letters and Speeches*, New York: Evert Springhorn, 1964, p. 176).
5. *A Doll's House* was first translated into English by T. Weber in 1880. Two years later another English version, superior to the previous one, was made by Mrs Henrietta Frances Lord. In the mid-eighties an adaptation of the play under the title *Breaking a Butterfly* was performed in London. However, it was not until William Archer's translation of the play and its performance at the Novelty Theatre in 1889 that Ibsen had a decisive reception in England. The play shocked the English audience as it shocked the French and German audiences, who had seen it earlier.

   After the three weeks' run of the play in June, Ibsen became notorious in England and he was attacked in the contemporary press. Bernard Shaw, who was introduced to him in the mid-eighties by his friend Archer, defended him vigorously in a lecture he gave in July 1890 to the Fabian Society. Most of the lecture was devoted to *A Doll's House* and out of this lecture emerged *The Quintessence of Ibsenism*—the first book in English about Ibsen.
6. Ibsen reacted strongly against the change which the German producers made at the end of the play when it was prepared for the stage and described it as a

'barbarous outrage'. (*Ibsen Letters and Speeches*, pp. 183–4)

In the same conversation with Clodd (mentioned above) Meredith said that 'as woman gets her emancipation she can dictate to men on more equal terms'.

7. Barbara Hardy, *Meredith Now*, p. 301.

8. The narrator similarly views Nataly's situation in connection with the social oppression of women: 'Men do not feel this doubtful position as women must. They have not the same to endure; the world gives them land to tread, where women are on breaking seas.' (VI, 51)

In the early draft of *The Amazing Marriage* we know that Fleetwood 'exulted being young and a man'. (*B*, 242)

9. *The Bookman* (Jan. 1896) p. 128.

10. *The Echo* (Nov. 1895) p. 1.

11. *The Pall Mall Gazette* (Nov. 1895) p. 5.

12. *The Globe* (Nov. 1895) p. 5.

13. M. Sturge Henderson, *George Meredith* (1907) p. 299.

14. Norman Kelvin, *A Troubled Eden*, p. 194.

15. In the course of her study of Meredith's novels Phyllis Bartlett apparently underestimates the role of Dame Gossip in the book, when she refers to her as a social commentator device of unnecessary complication in the narrative method designed to simplify narration. (*A Review of English Literature*, III (1962) p. 37)

16. Meredith might have derived the term from R. L. Stevenson's 'A Gossip on Romance', *Longman's Magazine* (Nov. 1882) pp. 69–79.

As a narrator Dame Gossip recalls the observer type of narrator used by Henry James and Joseph Conrad where events are rendered by the narrator as they came to him through observation or hear-say.

CHAPTER 7

1. Richard Le Gallienne, *George Meredith: Some Characteristics*, p. 179.

2. *The Yellow Book*, III (1894) p. 210.

3. *The Yellow Book*, V (1895) p. 175.

Street was unaware of the fact that the stories were first published in *The New Quarterly Magazine: The House on the Beach* in January 1877; *The Case of General Ople and Lady Camper* in July 1877; *The Tale of Chloe* in July 1879. The three stories were first reprinted in book form in America: the first in 1877, the second and the third in 1890. Another reprint of *The Tale of Chloe* was in 1891. The English edition appeared in 1894, and Street's reference is presumably to this edition (Ward, Lock and Bowden).

4. Ibid., pp. 180–1.

5. *The Yellow Book*, XIII (1897) p. 101.

6. W. G. Blakie Murdock, *The Renaissance of the Nineties* (1911) pp. 11–16.

7. Arthur Symons, 'A Note on George Meredith' in *Studies in Prose and Verse* (1904) p. 149.

In his review of Le Gallienne's book on Meredith (*The Academy*, January 1891, p. 81) Symons comments that Meredith is as conscious an artist as Goncourt 'with whom he may be compared for his experimental treatment of language, his attempt to express what has never been expressed before by forcing words to say more than they are accustomed to'.

8. Bernard Muddiman, *The Men of the Nineties* (1920) p. 55.
9. Nordau defines the *'fin de Siecle'* as 'a name covering both what is characteristic of many modern phenomena, and also the underlying notion as a practical emancipation from traditional discipline, which theoretically is still in force'. *Degeneration* (translated from the Second Edition of the German Work) (London: 1896) pp. 1–3. First appeared in 1893.

   Chronologically the term is established as a reference to the 1890s. However, it is often used to include the late years of the eighties, and I am using it here in this capacity but still without a definitive description.
10. Lord Henry wonders 'who it was defined man as a rational animal. It was the most premature definition ever given. Man is many things but he is not rational' (Oscar Wilde, *The Picture of Dorian Gray*, New York, 1954, p. 30).
11. Osbert Sitwell, 'The Novels of George Meredith', *The English Association: Presidential Address* (November 1947) p. 11.

    On one occasion Sitwell told Percy Colson that he preferred Meredith to Hardy and thought that *The Egoist* and *Diana of the Crossways* would outlast any of Hardy's novels (*Close of an Era*, 1945, p. 112).
12. It is sufficient to see two major critics of Meredith, Walter F. Wright and Jack Lindsay each devote only a few pages for *The Amazing Marriage*.
13. Jack Lindsay, op. cit., p. 313.
14. Barbara Hardy, *Meredith Now*, p. 295.
15. *Letters from George Meredith and Edward Clodd and Clement K. Shorter* (printed for private circulation, 1913) pp. 27–8.
16. *The Times Literary Supplement* (22 Oct. 1971) p. 1311.
17. Joseph E. Kruppa, 'Meredith's Late Novels: Suggestions for a Critical Approach', *Nineteenth Century Fiction*, ixx (1964) p. 285.

APPENDIX I

1. Bulwer-Lytton, *Miscellaneous Prose Works*, ii (1868) p. 154.
2. 'Preface to the Second Edition', *The Disowned*, i (1829) p. vi.
3. 'Preface to the Edition of 1840', *Ernest Maltravers* (1873) pp. 7–8.
4. W. F. Monypenny, *The Life of Benjamin Disraeli, 1804–1837*, i (1910) p. 236.
5. Benjamin Disraeli, *Vivian Grey*, i (1881) pp. 368–9.
6. Reporting Goethe's appreciation of *Vivian Grey*, Monypenny reports that Goethe and his daughter-in-law 'could find but one fault, that the author had misconceived the German character in his youthful Princess'. *The Life of Benjamin Disraeli*, i, p. 476.
7. *The Monthly Review; or Literary Journal, Enlarged*, remarks that *Wilhelm Meister* 'sketches a few years of the life of a strolling player, whose shifting acquaintance and unimportant adventures offer some variety of stimulant incidents, which have no other coherence than the unity of the hero'. (cvi, 1825, p. 528) Other current reviews were similarly concerned with the wanton adventurer (*Blackwood Edinburgh Magazine*, xv (1824) p. 623; *London Magazine*, x (1824) pp. 291–307). It is not until the sixties when reviews began to see in the book more than adventures and inconsistent immoral passion (*Atlantic Monthly* (Sept. 1865) pp. 273–82; (October 1865) pp. 448–57; *North American Review* (July 1865) pp. 281–5).

8. G. H. Lewes, *The Life and Works of Goethe*, I (1855) p. 210.
9. Charles Dickens, *David Copperfield*, II, Gadshill Edition (1897) p. 461.
10. F. R. and Q. D. Leavis, *Dickens the Novelist* (1970) p. 46.

APPENDIX III

1. *Anti-Jacobin* (25 April 1891) p. 311.
2. *The National Observer* (2 May 1891) p. 618.
3. *The Academy* (13 June 1891) p. 555.
4. *The Daily Chronicle* (22 April 1891) p. 8.
5. *Vanity Fair* (9 May 1891) p. 405.
6. *The Speaker* (9 May 1891) p. 561.
7. *The Times* (18 May 1891) p. 14.
8. *The Athenaeum* (2 May 1891) pp. 562–2.
9. *The Daily Telegraph* thinks that the fall with which the book opens is a commonplace event surrounded by 'the coruscations of those intellectual fireworks' (15 April 1891, p. 5). *The Glasgow Herald* sarcastically says that the 'stupendous sentence is not a literal translation from the German, neither is it quoted from any of those parodies of Mr. Meredith which have been recently indulged in'. (30 Apr. 1891, p. 9) *The Daily News* describes the breathless toil required before the relief of a period is to be found. (2 May 1891, p. 2) *The Saturday Review* quotes the first sentence (which it refers to as the first paragraph of the novel) with the comment: 'This surely is not the way to write' (23 May 1891, p. 626).
10. *Manchester Guardian* (28 Apr. 1891) p. 10.
11. *The Spectator* (May 1891) p. 763.
12. *The Pall Mall Gazette* (21 Apr. 1891) p. 3.
13. Richard Garnett, *The Illustrated London News* (2 May 1891) p. 571.
14. Richard Le Gallienne, *Meredithiana* (1924) p. 117. Forman draws upon Smith's quotation from Le Gallienne's book because it is the only explicit reference.
15. Richard Le Gallienne, *The Novel Review* (May 1892) pp. 149–50.
16. Richard Le Gaullienne, *George Meredith: Some Characteristics* (1905) pp. 188–9. For details about the composition of the book, see 'The Birth of a Book' in James G. Nelson's *The Early Nineties, A View from the Bodley Head* (Harvard University Press, 1971) pp. 111–25.

APPENDIX IV

1. *The Standard* (Nov. 1895) p. 2.
2. *The Realm* (Nov. 1895) p. 899.
3. *The Saturday Review* (Dec. 1895) p. 842.
4. *St. James Gazette* (Nov. 1895) p. 3.
5. *The Athenaeum* (Nov. 1895) p. 748.
6. *Publisher's Circular* (May 1896) p. 546.
7. *Daily Telegraph* (Nov. 1895) p. 7.
8. Siegfried Sassoon, *Meredith*, pp. 234–6.

Sassoon is probably misled by Meredith's frequent references to stylistic matters into crediting him with a greater concern for style than he in fact possessed. For details see D. S. Austin's 'Meredith on the Nature of Metaphor' (*University of Toronto Quarterly*, xxvii (1957) pp. 96–101).

9. Lionel Stevenson, *The Ordeal of George Meredith* (New York, 1953) p. 322.
10. Watter Wright, *Art and Substance in George Meredith*, p. 99.

Selected Bibliography

BOOKS

Allen, Grant, *The Woman Who Did* (1895)
Auchincloss, Louis, *Reflections of a Jacobite* (1961)
Beach, J. W., *The Comic Spirit in George Meredith* (1911)
Beer, Gillian, *Meredith: A Change of Masks* (1970)
Booth, Wayne C., *The Rhetoric of Fiction* (University of Chicago Press, 1966)
Booth, William, *In Darkest England and the Way Out* (1891)
Brown, Horatio F., *John Addington Symonds, A Biography*, 2 vols (1895)
Butler, Samuel, *The Way of All Flesh*, ed. D. F. Howard (1964)
Carlyle, Thomas, *Works*, Centenary Edition, 30 vols (1896)
Caudwell, Christopher, *Romance and Realism* (Princeton: 1970)
Clodd, Edward, *Memories* (1916)
Collins, Philip, *Dickens, The Critical Heritage* (1971)
Colson, Percy, *Close of an Era* (1945)
Comte, Auguste, *Positive Philosophy*, trans. by Harriet Martineau, 2 vols (1853)
Daiches, David, *A Critical History of English Literature*, iv (1968)
Dickens, Charles, *Works*, Gadshill Edition, 38 vols (1897–1908)
Disraeli, B., *Contarini Fleming*, 2 vols (1832)
——, *Sybil*, 3 vols (1845)
——, *Lothair*, 3 vols (1870)
——, *Vivian Grey* in *Novels and Tales*, 12 vols, Hughenden Edition (1881)
Eliot, George, *Felix Holt: The Radical*, 2 vols, Standard Edition (Edinburgh: 1895)
Ellis, S. M., *George Meredith: His Life and Friends in Relation to his Work* (1919)
Erskine, J., *The Delight of Great Books* (1928)
Fletcher, Ian, ed., *Meredith Now: Some Critical Essays* (1971)
Forster, E. M., *Aspects of the Novel* (1928)

Forster, John, *The Life of Charles Dickens*, new edition with notes and an index by A. J. Hoppé, 2 vols (1969)

Galsworthy, John, *The Man of Property* (1970)

Goethe, W. M., *Wilhelm Meister's Apprenticeship and Travels*, trans. by Thomas Carlyle, Standard Edition, VIII (1904). First appeared in 1824.

———, *Wilhelm Meister's Apprenticeship*, trans. by R. D. Boylan (1855)

———, *The Sorrows of Young Werther*, trans. by William Rose (1929)

Goodheart, Eugene, *The Cult of the Ego* (Chicago: 1968)

Gosse, Edmund, *Ibsen* (New York: 1907)

———, *Father and Son* (1967)

Gould, Frederick J., *Hyndman, Prophet of Socialism* (1928)

Graham, Kenneth, *English Criticism of the Novel: 1865–1900* (Oxford: 1965)

Griest, Guinevere L., *Mudie's Circulating Library and the Victorian Novel* (Indiana University Press, 1971)

Hardy, Barbara, *The Novels of George Eliot* (1963)

———, *The Appropriate Form* (1964)

———, ed., *Critical Essays on George Eliot* (1970)

Harvey, W. J., *Character and the Novel* (1966)

Howe, Susanne, *Wilhelm Meister and his English Kinsmen* (Columbia University Press, 1930)

Hyndman, H. M., *The Text-Book of Democracy: England For All* (1881)

———, *The Historical Basis of Socialism in England* (1883)

———, *The Social Reconstruction of England* (1884)

———, *The Coming Revolution in England* (1884)

———, *Commercial Crises of the Nineteenth Century* (1892)

———, *The Record of an Adventurous Life* (1911)

Ibsen, H., *Nora,* trans. by Henrietta Frances Lord (1882)

———, *A Doll's House*, trans. by William Archer (1889)

James, Henry, *The Letters of Henry James*, 2 vols, ed. Percy Lubbock (1920)

———, *The House of Fiction* (1957)

Jerrold, Walter, *George Meredith, an Essay Towards Appreciation* (1902)

Johnson, Diane, *Lesser Lives: The True History of the First Mrs Meredith and Other Lives* (1973)

Kelvin, Norman, *A Troubled Eden: Nature and Society in the Works of George Meredith* (Stanford University Press, 1961)

LaValley, Albert J., *Carlyle and the Idea of the Modern* (Yale University Press, 1968)

Lawrence, D. H., *Collected Letters*, 2 vols, ed. Harry T. Moore (1962)

Leavis, F. R. and Q. D., *Dickens the Novelist* (1970)

Le Gallienne, Richard, *George Meredith: Some Characteristics* (1905) first published in 1890

Lewes, G. H., *The Life and Works of Goethe*, 2 vols (1855)

——, *Female Characters of Goethe from the Original Drawings of William Kaulbach with Explanatory Text* (1867)

——, *Ranthorpe* (1842)

——, *The Apprenticeship of Life* (1850)

Lindsay, Jack, *George Meredith* (1956)

Lukacs, George, *The Historical Novel* (1969)

Lytton, Edward Bulwer-, *Pelham*, 3 vols (1829)

——, *The Disowned*, 3 vols (1829)

——, *Ernest Maltravers* (1873) first published 1837

——, *The Caxtons*, 3 vols (1849)

——, *Miscellaneous Prose Works*, 3 vols (1868)

Marx, Karl, and Frederick Engels, *On Britain* (Moscow: 1953)

Maxse, F. A., *National Education and its Opponents: a Lecture by Rear-Admiral Maxse* (1877)

——, *Woman Suffrage. The Counterfeit and the True Reasons for Opposing Both* (1877)

——, *The Causes of Social Revolt* (1872)

Meredith, George, *Works*, 27 vols, Memorial Edition (1909–11)

——, *The Adventures of Harry Richmond*, first edition, 3 vols (1871)

——, *The Adventures of Harry Richmond*, first revised edition (1886)

——, *The Adventures of Harry Richmond*, ed. L. T. Hergenhan (University of Nebraska Press, 1970)

——, *The Tale of Chloe – the House on the Beach – the Case of General Ople and Lady Camper* (Word, Lock & Bawden, 1894)

——, *The Letters of George Meredith*, ed. C. L. Cline, 3 vols (Oxford: 1970)

——, *Letters of George Meredith*, ed. William Maxse Meredith, 2 vols (1912)

——, *The Ordeal of Richard Feverel*, ed. C. L. Cline, Riverside Edition (Boston: 1971)

Mill, J. S., *Autobiography* (1875)

Miller, J. Hillis, *Charles Dickens: The World of his Novels* (Cambridge, Massachusetts: 1958)

Monypenny, W.F., *The Life of Benjamin Disraeli*, 6 vols (1910–1920)

142 *George Meredith*

Muddiman, Bernard, *The Young Men of the Nineties* (1920)
Murdoch, W. G., *The Renaissance of the Nineties* (1911)
Nelson, James G., *The Early Nineties: A View from the Bodley Head* (Harvard University Press, 1971)
Nordau, Max, *Degeneration*, Translated from the Second Edition of the German Work (1896)
Priestley, J. B., *George Meredith* (1926)
Pritchett, V. S., *The Working Novelist* (1965)
——, *George Meredith and English Comedy* (1970)
——, 'Introduction' to *The Egoist*, the Bodley Head Edition (1972)
Sassoon, Siegfried, *Meredith* (1948)
Seeley, J. R., *The Expansion of England* (1883)
Sencourt, Robert Esmonde, *The Life of George Meredith* (1929)
Shaw, Bernard, *The Quintessence of Ibsenism* (1913)
Sitwell, Osbert, *The Novels of George Meredith* in *The English Association* (Nov. 1947)
Spencer, Herbert, *Education* (1861)
——, *The Study of Sociology* (1874)
Spencer, Walter T., *Forty Years in my Bookshop* (1923)
Sprinchorn, Evert, *Ibsen, Letters and Speeches* (New York: 1964)
Stevenson, Lionel, *The Ordeal of George Meredith* (New York: 1953)
——, ed., *Victorian Fiction: A Guide to Research* (Harvard University Press, 1964)
Stone, Donald, *Novelists in a Changing World* (Harvard University Press, 1972)
Symonds, J. A., *Essays, Speculative and Suggestive*, 2 vols (1890)
Symons, Arthur, *Figures of Several Centuries* (1916)
Trollope, Anthony, *My Confidence* (1896)
Tsuzuki, C., *H. M. Hyndman and British Socialism* (Oxford, 1961)
Wells, H. G., *The Story of a Great Schoolmaster* (1924)
Whewell, William, *History of the Inductive Sciences* (1837)
——, *Philosophy of the Inductive Sciences: on the Philosophy of Discovery, Chapters Historical and Critical* (1860) first published 1840.
——, *Novum Organum Renovatum: Being the Second Part of the Philosophy of the Inductive Sciences* (1858) first published 1840.
Wilde, Oscar, *The Soul of Man Under Socialism* (1919)
——, *A Critic in Pall Mall: Being Extracts from Reviews and Miscellanies* (1919)
——, *Intentions* (1891)
——, *The Picture of Dorian Gray* (New York, 1954)
Williams, Ioan, ed., *Meredith: The Critical Heritage* (1971)

Wright, Walter F., *Art and Substance in George Meredith* (University of Nebraska Press, 1953)

Zola, Emile, *Money*, trans. by Ernest A. Vizetelly (1894)

ARTICLES AND REVIEWS

Austin, Deborah S., 'Meredith on the Nature of Metaphor', *University of Toronto Quarterly*, XXVII (1957) pp. 96–101.

Bartlett, Phyllis, 'Richard Feverel, Knight-Errant', *Bulletin of the New York Public Library* (July 1959) pp. 329–40

——, 'The Novels of George Meredith', *A Review of English Literature*, III (1962) pp. 31–46.

Baylon, Joseph O., and Patrick G. Hogan, Jr., 'W. T. Stead's "Interview with George Meredith": An Unpublished Version', *Tennessee Studies in Literature*, IX (1964) pp. 99–116.

Beer, Gillian, '*One of our Conquerors*: Language and Music' in *Meredith Now* (1970)

Brogan, Howard O., 'Fiction and Philosophy in the Education of Tom Jones, Tristram Shandy, and Richard Feverel', *College English*, XIV (1952) pp. 144–9.

Buckler, W., 'The Artistic Unity of "Richard Feverel" ', *Nineteenth Century Fiction*, VII (1952) pp. 119–24.

Cline, C.L., 'Meredith's Meeting with the Carlyles', *Times Literary Supplement* (9 Nov. 1973).

Clodd, Edward, 'Meredith's Conversations with Clodd, I', *Times Literary Supplement* (8 May 1953) p. 308.

Curtin, Frank D., 'Adrian Harley: The Limits of Meredith's Comedy', *Nineteenth Century Fiction*, VII (1953) pp. 272–89.

Edgar, Pelham, 'George Meredith', *The National Review* (Sept. 1907) pp. 61–81.

Ekeberg, Gladys W., ' "The Ordeal of Richard Feverel" as Tragedy', *College English*, VII (1946) pp. 387–93.

Eliot, George, 'The Natural History of German Life', *Westminster Review* (July 1856) pp. 51–79.

——, 'Silly Novels by Lady Novelists', *Westminster Review* (Oct. 1856) pp. 442–61.

——, *Westminster Review* (April, 1856) pp. 625–50.

Fagner, Donald, 'George Meredith as Novelist', *Nineteenth Century Fiction*, XVI (1962) pp. 317–29.

Fullerton, Morton, 'George Meredith', *The Yellow Book*, III (1894) p. 210.

Graber, Terry H., ' "Scientific" Education and Richard Feverel', *Victorian Studies*, XIV (1970) pp. 129–43.

Haight, Gordon S., 'George Meredith and the *"Westminster Review"* ' *Modern Language Review*, LIII (1958) pp. 1–16.

Hardy, Barbara, '*Lord Ormont and his Aminta* and *The Amazing Marriage*' in *Meredith Now*, pp. 295–312.

Hergenhan, L. T., 'Meredith's Revisions of Harry Richmond', *Review of English Studies*, XIV (1963) pp. 24–32.

——, 'Meredith's Attempts to Win Popularity: Contemporary Reactions', *Studies in English Literature: 1500–1900*, IV (1964) pp. 637–51.

——, 'The Reception of George Meredith's Early Novels', *Nineteenth Century Fiction*, XIX (1965) pp. 213–35.

——, 'Meredith Achieves Recognition: The Reception of *Beauchamp's Career* and *The Egoist*', *Texas Studies in Literature and Language*, XI (1969) pp. 1247–68.

Hudson, Richard B., 'Meredith's Autobiography and the *"The Adventures of Harry Richmond"*', *Nineteenth Century Fiction*, IX (1954) pp. 38–49.

Kettle, Arnold, '*Beauchamp's Career*' in *Meredith Now*.

Kruppa, Joseph E., 'Meredith's Late Novels: Suggestions for a Critical Approach', *Nineteenth Century Fiction*, XIX (1964) pp. 271–86.

Lane, John, 'Perils of the New Censorship. How "Richard Feverel" was banned. Meredith Letters. "O, Canting Age".' *The Observer* (12 Dec. 1909) p. 9.

——, 'Impressions', *The Bodleian* (January 1910) pp. 8–9.

Le Gallienne, Richard, 'Meredith for the Multitude', *The Novel Review* (Apr. 1892) pp. 140–52.

Lukacs, G., 'The Intellectual Physiognomy of Literary Characters', *International Literature*, VIII (1936) pp. 55–83.

McCarthy, Justine, 'Novels with a Purpose', *Westminster Review* (July 1864) pp. 24–49.

Meredith, George, *Westminster Review* (Apr. 1857) pp. 602–20.

Mitchell, Juliet, '*The Ordeal of Richard Feveral*: a Sentimental Education' in *Meredith Now*.

Milner, Viscountess, 'Talks with George Meredith', *The National Review*, CXXXI (1848) pp. 448–58.

Mortimer, Raymond, 'Encumbered by Genius', *The Sunday Times* (17 May 1970) p. 31.

Moynaham, Julian, 'The Hero's Guilt: the Case of *Great*

Expectations', *Essays in Criticism*, xx (1960) pp. 60–79.

Richards, Bernard A., *'One of Our Conquerors* and the Country of the Blue', in *Meredith Now*.

Robertson, John M., 'Concerning Preciosity', *The Yellow Book*, xiii (1897) pp. 79–106.

Russell, B., 'Byron and the Modern World', *A Journal of the History of Ideas*, i (1940) pp. 24–37.

Shaheen, M. Y., 'Forster on Meredith', *The Review of English Studies*, xxiv (1973) pp. 185–91.

——, 'On Meredith's Letters', *American Notes and Queries* (Jan. 1973) pp. 69–71.

Smith, Garnet, 'The Women of George Meredith', *The Fortnightly Review* (May 1896) pp. 775–90.

Stevenson, R. L., 'A Gossip on Romance', *Longman's Magazine* (Nov. 1882) pp. 69–79.

Street, G. S., 'Mr Meredith in Little', *The Yellow Book*, v (1895) pp. 174–85.

Tennyson, A., 'An Ode in Honour of the Jubilee of Queen Victoria' in *Macmillan's Magazine* (Apr. 1887) pp. 401–6.

Thomson, Fred C., 'Stylistic Revisions of *One of Our Conquerors*', *The Yale University Library Gazette*, xxxvi (1961) pp. 62–74.

MISCELLANEOUS

'Our Novels. The Sensational School', *The Temple Bar* (June 1870) pp. 410–24.

'The Battle of Dorking: Reminiscences of a Volunteer', *Blackwood's Magazine*, cix (1871) pp. 539–72.

'Light Literature', *Belgravia* (May 1873) pp. 328–35.

'Recent Novels', *The Times* (18 Aug. 1876) p. 4.

'Character Sketch: George Meredith', *The Review of Reviews* (Mar. 1904) pp. 225–30.

'Mr George Meredith on the Future of Liberalism. Home Rule and Imperialism', *Manchester Guardian* (2 Feb. 1903) p. 5.

'Meredith on the up', *Times Literary Supplement* (22 October 1971) p. 1311.

CONTEMPORARY REVIEWS

The Ordeal of Richard Feverel
  The Leader (2 July 1859) p. 798.
  The Spectator (9 July 1859) pp. 717–18.
  The Critic (2 July 1859) pp. 6–7.
  The Times (14 Oct. 1859) p. 5.

Harry Richmond
  The Queen (30 Dec. 1871) p. 440.
  The Australasian (10 Feb. 1872) p. 167.
  The Examiner (11 Nov. 1871) p. 1122.
  The Spectator (20 Jan. 1872) pp. 79–80.
  The Morning Post (2 Dec. 1871) p. 3.
  The Athenaeum (4 Nov. 1871) pp. 590–1.
  The Westminster Review (Jan. 1872) pp. 274–5.
  Time (Feb. 1886) n.s. xxv, pp. 247–8.
  The Daily Telegraph (20 Nov. 1871) p. 3.

Beauchamp's Career
  The Examiner (8 Jan. 1876) pp. 45–6.
  The Pall Mall Gazette (5 Feb. 1876) pp. 11–12.
  The British Quarterly Review (Apr. 1879) pp. 411–25.
  The Saturday Review (13 May 1876) pp. 626–7.
  The Canadian Monthly (Apr. 1876) pp. 341–3.
  The Academy (15 Jan. 1876) p. 51.

One of Our Conquerors
  The Anti-Jacobin (25 Apr. 1891) p. 311.
  The National Observer (2 May 1891) p. 618.
  The Academy (13 June 1891) pp. 555–6.
  The Daily Chronicle (22 Apr. 1891) p. 8.
  Vanity Fair (9 May 1891) p. 405.
  The Speaker (9 May 1891) pp. 560–1.
  The Times (18 May 1891) p. 14.
  The Athenaeum (2 May 1891) pp. 561–2.
  The Daily Telegraph (15 Apr. 1891) pp. 4–5.
  The Glasgow Herald (30 Apr. 1891) p. 9.
  The Daily News (2 May 1891) p. 2.
  The Saturday Review (23 May 1891) p. 626.

The Amazing Marriage
  The Bookman (Jan. 1896) p. 128.
  The Echo (28 Nov. 1895) p. 1.
  The Pall Mall Gazette (23 Dec. 1895) p. 4.
  The Globe (27 Nov. 1895) p. 5.
  The Standard (18 Nov. 1895) p. 2.
  The Realm (25 Nov. 1895) p. 899.
  The Saturday Review (21 Dec. 1895) p. 842.
  St. James Gazette (23 Nov. 1895) p. 3.
  The Athenaeum (30 Nov. 1895) p. 748.
  Publisher's Circular (16 May 1896) p. 546.
  The Daily Telegraph (22 Nov. 1895) p. 7.

Index

Meredith's published works are indexed alphabetically by title. Page-references in bold type indicate central discussion.